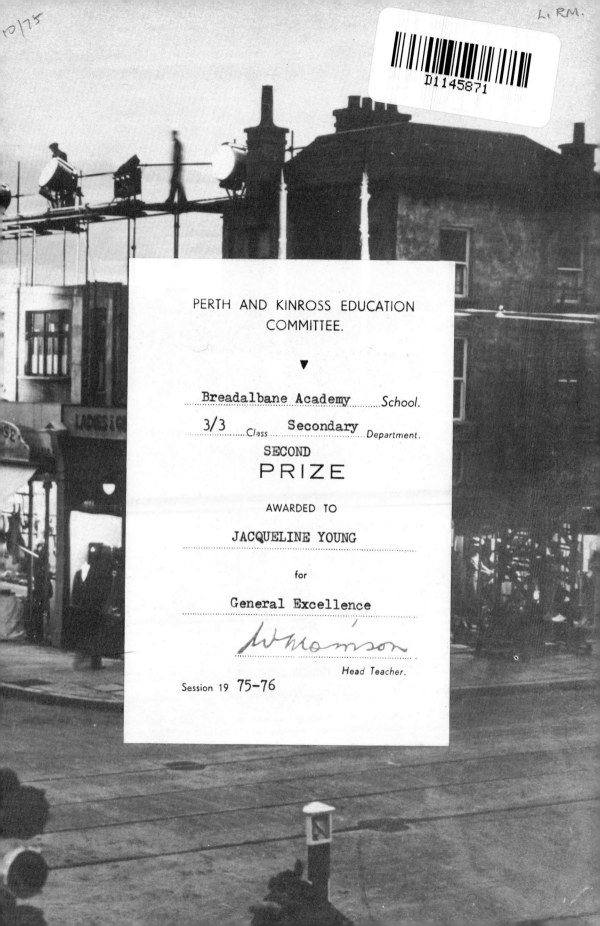

PERTH AND KINROSS EDUCATION
COMMITTEE.

▼

Breadalbane Academy ......School.

3/3 ....Class.... Secondary ....Department.

SECOND
PRIZE

AWARDED TO

JACQUELINE YOUNG

for

General Excellence

W Thomson

Head Teacher.

Session 19 75-76

Contents

ENDPAPER
A still that sums up what film-making is all about: the thrill of creating and preserving drama on celluloid, using natural locations but bending them to one's will. What you see is the making of an Alfred Hitchcock thriller as long ago as 1936, but the techniques have altered little. The street looks real until you see the lighting walkways at the top of the shell-like buildings; then you realize that it has all been built in the grounds of a London studio. It's a twilight scene, but without special help from the great lighting arcs nothing could be photographed. The whole set has been designed to meet the needs of the story; presumably no real street could be found with the necessary row of shops including a little cinema. This film is Sabotage, and it is still shown by film societies.

THE
CLAPPERBOARD
BOOK OF THE

CINEMA

Leslie Halliwell and Graham Murray

With a Foreword by Chris Kelly

Hart-Davis, MacGibbon   London

Foreword

The *Clapperboard* team has been presenting the programme to television viewers for the past four years and for all of us, this book is a very special event.

When we devised *Clapperboard*—the programme, we were aiming to do something never done properly before on television: to present a whole view of the cinema and its history as an art, a craft, an industry and, of course, an entertainment. We also decided to concentrate our programme on single aspects of film— instead of flitting haphazardly from one excerpt of a new release to the next. We tried to be serious without being stodgy; to excite interest without being oversensational, and to give a sense of a living tradition in the cinema, to be able to show, for instance, how a silent film made sixty years ago could influence the latest Hitchcock movie.

The many letters we receive from viewers, aged anything from seven to seventy, make us feel that we are on the right track. But the trouble with television is that it's all over so fast. *Clapperboard*, for instance, lasts only twenty-five minutes. So we thought it would be a good idea to make it all a bit more permanent with this first *Clapperboard* book. I have greatly enjoyed being associated with both the programme and the book and hope that you will share my enjoyment for some time to come.

Chris Kelly

Granada Publishing Limited
First published in Great Britain 1975 by Hart-Davis, MacGibbon Ltd
Frogmore, St Albans, Hertfordshire AL2 2NF and
3 Upper James Street, London W1R 4BP

Copyright © 1975 by Leslie Halliwell, Graham Murray and Granada Television Limited

ISBN 0 246 10814 2

Printed in Great Britain by William Clowes & Sons, Limited, London, Beccles and Colchester

Introduction

There is so much entertainment on hand these days that boys and girls are in danger of growing up taking it for granted. Television is available all our waking hours; most people have plenty of spending money and showmen are not slow to think of ways in which they might quickly spend it. Advertising, hire purchase and 'permissiveness' are geared to give us everything we want at the very moment we are impelled to want it.

This is not entirely a good idea. It is one thing to be comfortable and appreciate progress, quite another to despise the world around us because its wonders are so easily available. The best entertainment, in the long run, is provided by an active mind which never loses its capacity to wonder.

In the field of the cinema, youngest of the arts, the need for films to make money has resulted in a degradation of quality. During the last twenty years, showmen have dangled one sensation after another in front of us, visual and verbal shocks alternating with new technical processes, until we and the film industry are quite exhausted. Films take an enormous amount of money to make, and producers fear that they will not get their money back with films for the family, full of well-behaved people. (*The Sound of Music* is the occasional exception which proves the rule.) They used to, but that particular audience now stays at home and watches television. Young adults are thought to be the only market group which will go out and pay, in sufficient numbers, to see a film; and they are thought to want only shocks. So one kind of audience is forced away, and the other is soon supped full of horrors, so that the cinema audience continues to dwindle, and to meet their costs films have to be made ever more cheaply.

It is not hard to see the possibility that soon the cinema industry will cease to exist, apart from films made cheaply for TV and perhaps the occasional long-running blockbuster. Now, the cinema has had nearly eighty years of honourable history, mirroring in one way or another not only the eventful years of the twentieth century, but our hopes and fears about other ages; it has stimulated our senses and our imaginations, and most grown-ups are able to think of a few key films in their young lives which have been very important to their later development.

Such an influential art (or craft, if you prefer) is worth the attention of the coming generations: in a way, cinema itself is living history. The weekly programme 'Clapperboard' was devised for those children who are prepared to think about films rather than simply sit through them and be either bored or entertained. We have put on programmes explaining special effects and technical processes, detailing the work of people behind the scenes, tracing the history of certain kinds of film, interviewing actors, directors and executives with something to say. (To no one's great surprise, our audience of adults, previously starved of such information, is almost as numerous as the young audience for which the programme is intended.)

This is the spirit we have tried to transfer to paper in this, the first of a series of 'Clapperboard' books. It is not a book to skim through for the sake of the pictures, which are all in black and white and chosen for their content rather than their prettiness; it is a book to read. It will appeal, we hope, to boys who like to take watches apart and see how they tick, and also to girls who adore *Alice in Wonderland*. In form it is a miscellany of separate pieces, long and short, on different aspects of cinema, some about people, some about processes, some about themes. It won't tell you everything you may want to know about the movies, but we hope it will stimulate your thinking. If there is any subject you would like us to tackle next time, please write to us c/o the publisher. Meanwhile, enjoy yourselves in the big, wide, wonderful world of cinema history.

Harold Lloyd, cinema's most famous comic stuntman who performed his extraordinary 'cliff-hangers' without the obvious aid of a safety net.

A Note on Film Appreciation

Cinema is sometimes known as the seventh art—the other six being painting, sculpture, music, ballet, writing, and photography. If cinema sometimes appears a little childish, that seems fair enough, as most of the others have been flourishing for three thousand years or so, whereas cinema cannot be said to have begun until 1895, when the Lumière brothers gave their first professional demonstration of the new apparatus in Paris. (There are other contenders for the privilege of being first: read a good history if the origins interest you.)

The problem of comparing cinema with the other arts is that so many people are involved: actors, producer, director, photographer, writer, editor, property master, art designer, continuity girl, assistant director, and up to a hundred others, including stunt men and doubles for the stars. Who is the main contributor, out of all these? To whom should the blame be attached for a bad film, or the praise for a good one?

Modern critics have singled out the director, but he is very often only one of a team. The appeal of the films of John Ford, for instance, depends very largely on actors like John Wayne, writers like Dudley Nichols, and photographers like Gregg Toland and Arthur Miller. The editor, especially in action films, plays an important part when he chooses which shots of each scene should be used, and how long each shot should be held. This is done on a workbench after all the film has been shot and the director has moved on to something else. Comedy too depends very often on reaction shots and precise timing, which is judged by the editor unless the film is shot in very long takes controlled by the actors. In a thriller, the music may be of prime importance for building up suspense and chilling one to the marrow. Only when all these talents come together at somewhere near their peak is the result likely to be a satisfying film.

The only director who has regularly controlled all these facets and therefore has only himself to blame is Alfred Hitchcock, who has been regarded as a law unto himself and plans every shot of his films before production starts, designing every detail of each scene in a long series of drawings called a 'storyboard'. Very few directors have had that kind of power; and even Hitchcock has frequently had his endings changed by the 'front office'.

Perhaps because of this confusion of responsibility, and the fact that many good films are good by accident, there has been a lack of simple introductions to the art. Quite the reverse: highbrow critics have tended to credit master craftsmen like Hitchcock with absurd artistic pretensions they never dreamed of. You are unlikely to find two histories of the cinema which agree precisely on any one contributor's talent, though eventually certain 'giants' appear, often because they stay the course longer than anyone else, or because they produce one lucky masterpiece and then die before their inability to follow it up can be revealed.

Each new student of the cinema brings his own problems, because at an early age he will have been impressed by certain films, different from those which have impressed anyone else, and films are not easily recalled for viewing in sufficient quantity for common judgments to be agreed upon. Another question which has to be decided, at least in one's own mind, is whether cinema is simply an entertainment—a film, something to be seen once for relaxation and then forgotten—or a pure art form like the others, seeking to express some essential truth in addition to providing the pleasure of professionalism in visual storytelling. The answer is of course that some films strive and succeed, others strive and fail, some do not strive at all, and others would have been better not made. In the long run it is up to you to judge.

Shirley Temple, the world's most famous child star.

The Great Ziegfeld, made in 1936 when musicals were really spectacular.

Errol Flynn, swashbuckler extraordinary, in Captain Blood, 1935.

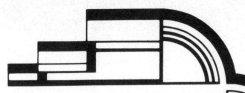

Unless you are a regular attender at one of the National Film Theatres you will see most of your old films on television, where they are usually presented in no sort of order, or in seasons which are incomplete because they are conditioned by what films are available at the time. Once in a blue moon you may see a silent film, often in extract, but most of the films on view will have been made since 1927 when the 'talkies' came in, and these days regrettably few films of the thirties are revived. The forties provided both the peak and the last gasp of the studio system, when cinema-going was cheap and popular and studios maintained vast rosters of talent. After 1950 the talent itself got the upper hand and each production tended to start from scratch, mainly on location, which meant more mishaps and the loss of the viewer's ability to place individual films within a studio's output, which had often provided a useful starting point for comparison. (Most of us who are old enough to remember the forties could walk into a cinema and know from the style of photography alone whether we were watching an MGM, Fox, Paramount or Warner film.)

Experiments with colour were made as long ago as 1898, and in the thirties it became reliable enough for use in occasional action pictures and musicals, but it was expensive. Not until the late sixties did it become absolutely standard, and then only because TV was moving into colour. Remember too, that TV does not show any film in the manner intended: watching an 18-inch picture in your living room with some lights on provides a different experience from watching a huge screen with two thousand other people in a darkened cinema. TV also crops the edges off all films, as you can tell from the credit titles; films made specifically for TV sensibly keep all essential action towards the middle of the picture area.

Until 1952 films were shot in the same picture ratio (i.e. comparative height and width) as television provides, but after that all normal films were intended to be shown on wider screens with the top and bottom of the image eliminated; these waste top and bottom areas are still present on TV. Films shot in the extremely wide systems like CinemaScope and Panavision cannot be shown satisfactorily on TV, although special versions are usually made by going back to the laboratory and choosing the most important picture areas from each scene. This obviously destroys the original composition, which can be just as damaging to the effect of a film as it would be if one trimmed a couple of inches from each edge of the Mona Lisa.

These are just a few of the pitfalls in view if you are a willing student who respects professionalism. If you are a wide-eyed revolutionary who thinks that the message is the thing and all film should be shot in grainy 8-mm with every shot running as long as it would take in life, then a whole new set of standards is required...and this book is probably not for you.

Acknowledgement

The illustrations are drawn from a wide variety of sources. The ownership of films frequently changes, and sometimes it is impossible to say who has control of pictorial publication rights, so we apologize if we have failed to secure any approvals. To all our sources we offer grateful thanks, but especially to the Walt Disney organization, EMI Film Productions, Columbia, Paramount, MGM, Warner, Twentieth-Century Fox, MCA/Universal, the Pathé Film Library, United Artists, and other principal producers and distributors.

THE FILM-GOING KELLY FAMILY

Chris Kelly presides each week over Granada's 'Clapperboard'—a programme about films for the family. And, off-screen, he also presides over his own family of film-addicts. Chris and his wife Vivien often take their children—Nicholas, twelve, and Rebecca, nine—to the pictures.

What kind of films do they like? Chris is particularly fond of foreign films, and he is a great fan of directors François Truffaut, Ingmar Bergman and Louis Malle. Vivien likes 'anything and everything—provided it's good'. She particularly likes thrillers—and the work of Alfred Hitchcock. 'The only thing I don't like is violence', she says. 'Chris has to go and see violent films without me. I did see "Soldier Blue" with him, but the violence in that upset me. I hated it.' Their little daughter Rebecca is a Walt Disney fan and enjoys all his old classics as well as his newer films. But the Kelly with the most surprising taste in films is young Nicholas.   He likes all the old silent comedies. And his favourite film stars? 'Charlie Chaplin, Buster Keaton and Laurel and Hardy.'

Two-faced Chris Kelly.
Film make-up expert Charles Parker goes to work on Chris in Granada's 'Clapperboard'. The photo shows Chris before and after...

HOLLYWOOD, THE FILM FACTORY

Movieland's Magic City

Probably Hollywood means less to young people these days than it did thirty or forty years ago. Then it lived in all our thoughts as a magic factory where dreams were made. From fan magazines we knew it well. The sun always shone outside, everyone had a swimming pool, there was no poverty (certainly not among the servants of stars) and the landscape generally gave every indication that the promised land had been found. Inside, the world's greatest writers could be summoned (and misused) at the command of a telephone call, and technicians stood by ready to create for the cameras every movie landscape from New York skyscrapers in a thunderstorm to a sun-kissed South Sea island.

Those were the golden days, when cinemas always had a queue outside and the movie business was virtually controlled by the owners of half a dozen big Hollywood studios whose only job was to manufacture elaborate fantasies. In

Metro-Goldwyn-Mayer Studios, for years the best known in Hollywood, were never very glamorous to look at. This factory-like view of them in their heyday shows the narrow pedestrian walks between the huge sound stages. The famous canteen or commissary, where all the stars ate lunch, is the nearest building on the right; it still serves the chicken soup which tycoon Louis B. Mayer made famous.

more recent years cameras have become more mobile and air travel quicker, so the craft of the studio has been scorned in favour of genuine locations all over the world (which are often less effective dramatically). The big studios gradually lost control to the individual directors and stars, who operate much more wastefully because they have to set up each production afresh; and in any case fewer films are now required to fill a rapidly dwindling number of cinemas around the world. It is not surprising

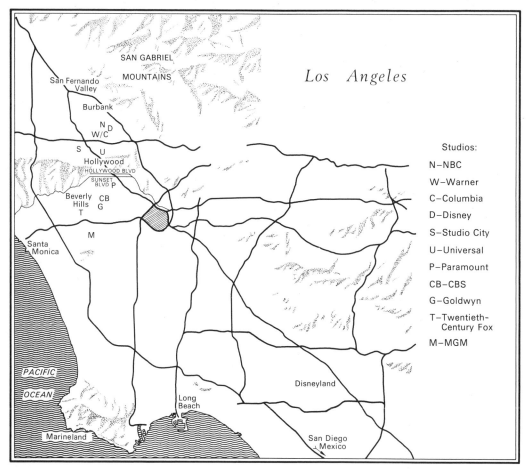

Studios:

N – NBC

W – Warner

C – Columbia

D – Disney

S – Studio City

U – Universal

P – Paramount

CB – CBS

G – Goldwyn

T – Twentieth-
Century Fox

M – MGM

This map covers an area approximately forty miles across, and it is all Los Angeles. The Hollywood area, which spreads far wider than the suburb of Hollywood itself, is shown by the letters which represent the major studios (see key above). The city centre, such as it is, is known as 'downtown', and few people from Hollywood go there: it's the shaded area in the centre. The thick lines are freeways, or, as we would say, motorways; without these, Los Angeles traffic would snarl up at thousands of traffic lights, and it is often quicker to travel thirty miles by a roundabout freeway route than eight or nine along ordinary streets. At the top left-hand corner is the once fabled San Fernando Valley, now totally suburbanized. Disneyland, bottom right, is an hour's fast driving from Hollywood proper.

that Hollywood is often referred to as a ghost town: the days of its glory are long ago, and there are very few monuments to its grandeur.

Before all the signs are erased completely by the building of new office blocks, let us take you for a tour of this strange landscape. Hollywood is officially one of the many suburbs of Los Angeles, one of the biggest cities in the world in surface area (they don't build upwards much because of the fear of earthquakes). LA, as everyone calls it, is in southern California, on the western coast of the United States, over six thousand miles from London and eleven hours fast flying time by direct route over the North Pole. (Thirty years ago the journey took nearly two weeks by ship and train via New York.) Los Angeles gets roughly the same seasonal daylight hours as we do, but its climate is much more appealing–some say the best in the world, if you like long hours of sun but also have to work occasionally. Winters are warm by our standards, snow being almost unknown; summers are hot but not humid. There is a fair amount of rain all the year round, but it comes in short bursts. Pleasantly, even on the hottest day there is usually cool relief in the evening. This is obviously an ideal climate for making films, sunny and reliable, which is why the first film-makers migrated to California from New York. (*Nothing* in Hollywood is older than 1915.) There is also a wide range of locations within a day's drive, from the hot deserts of Mojave and Death Valley to the snow-capped peaks of Mount Whitney and Yosemite (pronounced Yo-sem-ity). The disadvantage is that Los Angeles lies in a basin which often traps car fumes and causes a nasty, thick, choky smog. When it comes down, the wide straight streets take on the appearance of Sherlock Holmes's Baker Street in a pea-souper, and within half an hour your aching eyes, throat and chest make you give up regarding California as the promised land.

Someone called Los Angeles seventy-two suburbs in search of a city. Because each building needs its adjacent car park (you can't get anywhere in LA without a car, there being few buses and no Underground) the city spreads wider and wider. It is now over fifty miles square and mostly very ugly, the buildings being pale and rather dull unless they are built in fake Spanish style. (*Interior* decoration is what matters in California.) In the east LA stretches its ruthless tentacles into the desert; in the south and west it is mercifully bounded by the sea; in the north it long ago crossed the temporary

A street in the back lot of MGM studios. If you had but known, you might have recognized these fake buildings, usually serving as New York, from many a film you've seen on television. There is nothing behind the façades: interiors are shot in the sound stages, then linked in with the exterior shooting. The framework on top is there for special camera angles or lighting, and the tripods on the ground are to give additional light when even California's almost constant sunshine is insufficient. Sad to say, this fantasy street has now been torn down to make way for yet another group of high-rise apartment buildings: in future, when an MGM director wants to shoot a New York scene he will have to shoot it in New York.

This is what the MGM studios looked like in the very early twenties, before Goldwyn and Mayer were added to Metro. Although the criss-cross roads were laid out, there seem to be no other buildings around; but before long the whole area of Culver City was a mass of concrete, and in 1973 MGM decided that the land they owned was much more valuable for resale as real estate than maintained as a film studio.

On the other side of Hollywood from MGM—more than ten miles away—is Universal, which also has a long history dating back to 1915. But the studios have never been so busy as they are today. The reason is television: the executives at Universal seem to have had the best knack for making deals with the television networks and so keeping their studios filled with series like 'Columbo', 'Ironside' and 'Macmillan and Wife'. (They also make movies such as Airport.) Universal is now the only place you can go in Hollywood to capture a taste of former glories: its black tower seems to set an air of efficiency, the manner of its executives is keen and crisp, and its back lot is superbly maintained. Even the village sets used in 1931 for Frankenstein are still in use, and up on a hill stands the forbidding Bates mansion from Psycho. Incidentally, the row of sound stages in the far distance marks the Warner studio, and Disney is just a little way beyond.

interruption of the Hollywood hills and entrenched itself in the once-fertile San Fernando Valley, now like its parent a wilderness of hot dog stands, petrol stations and generally horrendous urban sprawl. Almost throughout this vast area the roads are ramrod straight, sometimes for thirty miles, and every traffic-lighted crossroads looks much the same as the previous one. There are few open spaces, and scarcely any of the districts, which run into each other without pause for greenery, have any style. Somewhere in the middle is the city centre known as 'downtown', but few people go there except to pay their taxes: it is notable only for vast new civic buildings and a 'spaghetti' junction of interweaving motorways. It also has its Chinatown, Little Tokyo, a Mexican street for tourists, a

railway station that looks like a cathedral, and a street of cinemas showing treble features twenty-four hours a day. About seven miles to the north, the last east–west street before the mountain canyons take over is Hollywood Boulevard, three miles long and as straight as an arrow. The central mile of it, only fifty years ago the nucleus of a community of orange-growers, is where thousands of tourists now stroll past wax museums and paltry gift shops, but not where the Hollywood action is. Only two of the famous studios, Columbia and Paramount, were ever sited in Hollywood itself, and they stand a mile or two south-east, on either side of the cemetery. Columbia has already been sold for redevelopment. MGM and Fox are roughly six miles south-west; Universal is two miles north over the hills; Warners, Disney and the new Columbia are further still, in Burbank. You would never notice them unless you particularly sought them out, and indeed there is little to see except bare, bland walls unless you are a privileged visitor and can be taken in to see the street on which Cagney and Bogart once shot it out, or Greta Garbo's dressing room (it looks just like any other).

The exception is Universal, which has lately made a huge tourist attraction of its facilities. For an admission fee of four dollars the tourist can kid himself that he has seen the inside of a movie studio. He drives through a special entrance next to the studio proper, and ascends via a steep new road to the top of a conical hill, where something like a fairyland funfair glistens in the sunshine. He is met by a pretty hostess, who introduces him to a gentleman dressed up as the Phantom of the Opera and then sends him off through a series of sideshows. Starting with a museum of Hollywood's past, he can watch stunt men falling off a roof, animate a Frankenstein model, cause snow to fall on a farm scene, and sip a drink on a terrace overlooking a splendid panoramic view of the backlot with its western streets and Psycho house. When he has had his fill of these pleasures he boards a gay little pink tram which takes him down the hill and very quickly once round the back lot, where if he is very lucky he may glimpse someone actually shooting a scene; after this he is firmly deposited at the car park.

It's a pleasant enough diversion on a fine day, and who can quarrel with success? The Universal tour is California's number two tourist attraction. (The first is San Simeon, palatial home of W. R. Hearst and the model for Xanadu in *Citizen Kane*.)

The other studios are disappointing to the casual visitor even if he can get in, as most have sold off their fascinating set-littered back lots for real estate. The outdoor structures which survive are depressingly broken down, except for the million dollar New York street built by Fox for *Hello Dolly*, which lines and decorates the main approach. It would be expensive to dismantle and so, since it's not in the way, has been left in all its fading splendour to fill the office of a car park. None of the studios is exactly a hive of activity, unless a TV series is shooting; 'real' movies are mostly shot on location these days apart from the finishing

TOP *On the right of the last picture is a green hill, much used for location shooting, and for a few dollars tourists can spend a happy day up there in a kind of funfair which includes restaurants, a cinema museum, an open air amphitheatre for stage shows, and various press button exhibitions where without fear or fuss one can make snow fall, bring a monster to life, shake hands with the Phantom of the Opera, or, as these people are doing, take a ride in the chariot used in* The Ten Commandments.

MIDDLE *Another tourist attraction is a stunt man display. The gentleman falling off the roof does so a dozen times a day to please spectators; but note the trampoline on to which he falls. You would not of course be allowed to see that if the scene were being shot for a movie.*

BOTTOM *When all the delights of the funfair have palled, a gay pink tram takes visitors round the studio back lot, where, if they are very lucky, a film may be shooting. In any case they see the Western street, watch a submarine being torpedoed, inspect a cowboy fort, see a house perpetually on fire and finally pass through a most spectacular effect, the parting of the Red Sea. By a mysterious process owing something to suction, the smooth waters of a man-made lake part before your very eyes, and your tram trundles through before the waters close up again behind you.*

touches. Last year we visited in the course of a week every studio in Hollywood, and found not a single film being shot in any of them. The British studios were busier.

The Disney studio is an exception of sorts, in that the cameras keep turning on modest live-action films, and a cartoon feature is always in some stage of preparation in the back rooms. The streets are still labelled Mickey Street and Dopey Drive, but the place has the general air of a small factory that has seen better days. The showmanship is reserved for Disneyland, thirty miles away; this mammoth funfair is a real cavalcade of wonders which gave us our most exciting day in America. Expensive to enter, but worth every penny for those who can appreciate professionalism, it's really aimed at intelligent adults: children get bored in less than half the time it takes to sample its delights.

The land is divided into impeccably recon-structed areas depicting New Orleans, the Wild West, or the main street of a turn-of-the-century small town. A train takes you on a quick trip round all of them, including a Mississippi steamboat and an Indian attack, and throws in a few animated dinosaurs for good measure. Then you are on your own with a book of tickets for the various rides: the Submarine Voyage, the African Cruise, the Haunted House, the Pirates of the Caribbean. Every one of them is better than you would expect from sampling any other pleasure garden: the mechanical ingenuity is unparalleled, the style of presenta-tion perfect. In a sense it is Disneyland which has distilled all the old magic of Hollywood and put it on permanent show: the film factories themselves are left to sigh for the better days gone by.

Apart from Universal, Hollywood can never have been the breathtaking place you may have been led to believe by films like The Jones Family in Holly-woo d; *there is no sight sufficiently exhilarating to cause the smiles on the faces of these actors, who are in fact looking the wrong way to see the gaudy*

façade of Grauman's Chinese Theatre, where a lot of posh premières used to take place. The theatre is the one touristy building on a long, dreary street. Knowing the district fairly well we can tell you that the Jones family are gazing with rapture at a gloomy old bank. Who says the camera never lies?

HOW
THE MOVIES
BEGAN

That moving pictures are possible at all is due to the fact that our eyes are able to retain for a fraction of a second the images, or pictures, which they receive when we look at things around us. This remarkable ability is called 'persistence of vision', and if you have a camera with a flash attachment it can be demonstrated very simply. Stand in a completely darkened room; hold one arm in front of you and with the other hand fire off a flashbulb, then quickly move the arm in front of you down to your side: you will for a moment or two see the arm still in its first position, even though it's not really there at all.

Because the successive pictures recorded by our vision overlap, each one slowly fading to be in turn replaced by the next one, a series of still pictures can be given the illusion of movement. Suppose we draw a number of pictures of a man walking, with his legs in a slightly different position each time, and then quickly flick the different drawings in front of our eyes, the man will appear to move his legs. You may have made similar drawings on the corner of each page in a book.

A Belgian professor named Joseph Plateau experimented with persistence of vision and in 1837 he invented a scientific toy which he called the

ABOVE *The Zoetrope. One of the nineteenth century scientific toys which produced the illusion of movement. In the illustration, part of the drum has been removed to show the drawn picture strip. By spinning the drum and looking through the slits the pictures appeared to move.*

BELOW *Part of the Zoetrope picture strip showing two boxers. Various strips were available, allowing a change of 'programme', and showed such things as horses galloping, acrobats and jugglers.*

'phantascope'. It consisted of a wheel containing a number of narrow vertical slits which was turned in front of a mirror. On the mirror side of the wheel there were drawings of people or animals in different positions. When the wheel was turned the drawings, viewed through the slits, appeared to move. A number of other similar toys, all using the principle of persistence of vision, were made during the nineteenth century and several of them can be seen and operated in the South Kensington Science Museum in London. All these devices depended of course on hand-drawn pictures. It was the invention of photography round about 1840 which was to lead to these 'toys' developing into the movie camera and projector.

In 1877, to settle a bet, a well-known photographer, Eadweard Muybridge, set up an experiment on a racecourse in California to see whether or not a galloping horse at any time lifted all its four feet off the ground together. He put up twenty-four cameras in a row; each camera was one foot apart, and attached to each shutter was a thread which ran across the track. As the horse galloped down the track it broke the threads and operated the shutter of each camera in turn. In this way Muybridge produced a series of photographs showing the various positions of a galloping horse, and showing incidentally that it did lift all four feet off the ground at one point. If Muybridge had been able to project his separate photographs one after the other quickly enough he would have had a moving picture of a horse galloping, but this was impossible with the glass plates on which photographs were taken in those days.

ABOVE *Edison's Kinetoscope. A continuous band of film, about 50 feet in length, was threaded around the various rollers. The viewer looked through a magnifying glass in the top of the box directly onto the film.*

BELOW *'Baby's Breakfast'. One of the films included in the Lumière Brothers first programme. The man in the picture is Auguste Lumière.*

Before permanent cinema buildings existed, travelling film shows became a popular feature of fun fairs. This is the 'Royal Electric' Bioscope, photographed in 1902 and owned by a showman named Walter Haggar. On the right of the picture you can see the steam engine which provided the electricity for the projector.

Using a battery of twenty-four cameras was very cumbersome, and the next big advance came when a Frenchman named E. Marey devised a camera which he called a 'photographic gun'. This had a circular disc holding a number of glass photographic plates, which rotated behind the camera lens. Marey used it to record amongst other things the phases of a seagull's flight. He also built a simple projection machine so that he could show the pictures. It was the introduction of celluloid instead of glass plates for taking photographs that made moving pictures a practical proposition.

By the 1880s a number of inventors in different parts of the world were simultaneously, and unknown to each other, all experimenting with ways of producing moving pictures using rolls of celluloid film, so it is not really possible to say that any one person 'invented' moving pictures. One of the more important, however, was an Englishman named William Friese-Greene, who was born in Bristol in 1855. He became a professional

photographer with a studio in Bath, and experimented with various devices based on persistence of vision. Eventually in June 1889 he patented 'a camera for producing a series of photographic images in rapid succession upon a celluloid film'. With this camera he filmed scenes in Hyde Park, which he projected at a photographic convention in Chester the following year. Friese-Greene's patent for a movie camera is certainly the earliest on record, and his demonstration at Chester appears to be the first ever projection of moving pictures to an audience. Unfortunately, Friese-Greene was a poor businessman and not only failed to make any money out of his invention but eventually spent practically everything he had on this and his other inventions, which included colour film. When he died in 1921 at a meeting of film producers in London they found only a few pence in his pocket. In 1951 the British Film Industry, as its contribution to the Festival of Britain, made a film of his life story with Robert Donat playing the part of William Friese-Greene. It was called *The Magic Box*.

At about the same time as Friese-Greene was patenting his camera in England, Thomas Alva Edison, who already had many inventions to his credit including the electric light bulb and the phonograph (or gramophone), was experimenting in the United States along similar lines to Friese-Greene. Edison produced a machine called the kinetoscope, a sort of peepshow which produced moving pictures but which could only be viewed by one person at a time. It was this machine which gave two Frenchmen, the Lumière brothers, their idea for a projector to show moving pictures to a large number of people at the same time.

In December 1895 the two brothers opened the world's first cinema in the basement of a café in Paris, showing a programme of short films they had made with a camera of their own design. The film consisted of very simple subjects such as 'Baby's Breakfast', 'The Blacksmith' and 'The Arrival of a Train at a Station'. This latter film appeared to be so realistic to their audiences that some people were quite frightened by it, imagining that the train on the screen was going to come right amongst them. In the following February the Lumière brothers visited London and at the Regent Street Polytechnic gave the first public show in this country to a paying audience. On the same day, 20 February 1896, a few miles away at Finsbury College, another English inventor, Robert W. Paul, was also demonstrating moving pictures with a projector he had made. Within a short time film shows were to become a regular part of the entertainment on music hall bills and at fun fairs. Soon showmen were renting empty shops and small halls to give film shows. These were the first cinemas, or 'picture palaces' as they quickly became known.

The movies had arrived.

ABOVE *A music hall bill of 1896 with Thomas Edison's Vitascope included as part of the programme. Regarded just as a passing novelty at the time, it was the cinema, in later years, which was to be largely responsible for the death of music hall.*

Elementary, my dear Watson

Sherlock Holmes on the Screen

Since Edgar Allan Poe created Dupin in the 1840s, many of our fictional folk heroes have been detectives. James Bond, for instance, is a spy detective; and generations of young people have thrilled to the adventures of Sexton Blake, Dixon Hawke, Dick Tracy, Hercule Poirot and Lord Peter Wimsey. The reason for the popularity of such figures is not far to seek. Primarily there is the interest of watching them solve a mystery: if well done, this is the most satisfying of all story forms, with a beginning, a middle and a surprising end. Then there is the action of the chase, and in good detective stories this always results from action of the mind; so vicariously the reader's brain and body are exercised at the same time. If in addition the writer can create an amusing and absorbing background, and characters that make you want to read about them again, he is home and dry.

All these elements are to be found in abundance in the stories of the world's most popular detective, Sherlock Holmes, created by Arthur Conan Doyle in 1887. Conan Doyle was then a struggling doctor who based his main character on a teacher of his, Joseph Bell, who stressed to his medical students the power of deduction, which really means building up the maximum information about something from the clues offered, which may not at first sight appear to be clues at all. Thus Sherlock Holmes could tell from looking at a watch that its owner was a

'The best Sherlock Holmes'—Basil Rathbone, pictured here with Nigel Bruce as Dr Watson, first took over the role and made it his own in the 1939 version of The Hound of the Baskervilles, *most filmed of all the Holmes stories. In appearance and manner he was obviously the perfect actor for the job, and seemed to enjoy the crisp rejoinders and frequent disguises which the part called for; yet a few years and thirteen films later he declared himself bored with the role and never played it again on screen.*

well-to-do man who had made several descents into poverty and finally become a drunkard. Like Conan Doyle's plots, his deductions don't always hold water under careful analysis; but almost immediately the character of his consulting detective, though never very carefully defined, caught on tremendously with the public, who defined him for themselves, with the help of illustrators, as hawk-nosed, piercing-eyed, middle-aged and given to going about in a deerstalker hat and an Inverness cape, a curved pipe clenched between his teeth and a magnifying glass in his hand. You will not find this image in Conan Doyle, but it is the image which has stuck.

For nearly a hundred years now, Sherlock Holmes has been a household name throughout the world. The fifty-six short stories and four novels in which he appears have been translated into every language, and there is a really splendid

This atmospheric view from the gate of Baskerville Hall shows Nigel Bruce as Watson with Richard Greene as Sir Henry. The mist is useful not only for providing atmosphere but to disguise the studio rocks; for this is an indoor set.

This third scene from The Hound of the Baskervilles *shows Holmes on the scent, questioning a cabby (E. E. Clive). The bearded gentleman is Lionel Atwill as Dr Mortimer, acting so sinister that he can't possibly be the villain.*

Arthur Wontner, the most elderly screen Holmes but one of the most satisfying, is seen among his chemicals in The Sign of Four *(1932).*

annotated edition which includes every known illustration from the original texts as well as copious information on all aspects of Victorian life touched on in the stories–a real desert island book. The notes treat Holmes and his friend and chronicler Dr Watson as though they were real people, and every incident in the stories is carefully dated by inference, the conclusions often being at variance with Conan Doyle's facts in the stories, which are sometimes slapdash in detail. The Annotated Sherlock Holmes is a kind of compendium of the work of Sherlock Holmes Societies around the globe, notably the American branch known as The Baker Street Irregulars: members of these clubs meet regularly to discuss Sherlock's love of music, his taste in women, his early life, just as though he were a real person. It produces for them a sophisticated kind of fun, and communicates the great enjoyment which the stories have given them. Conan Doyle's son Adrian joined in the make-believe and, with John Dickson Carr, wrote a dozen pastiche stories which have been added to the canon; he also turned his castle in Switzerland into a Holmes Museum. London boasts its own museum of Holmesiana; not in Baker Street, where the detective supposedly lived, but in the Sherlock Holmes public house at Charing Cross.

Sherlock Holmes became a famous stage character in 1899 when a celebrated American actor, William Gillette, wrote and acted in a play about him, called simply *Sherlock Holmes*. It was so popular that Gillette continued to play it for the rest of his life. (He also made a film of it in 1916.) In more recent years, however, despite attempts by Conan Doyle himself, Holmes has not been a popular stage figure, though he has, unbelievably, appeared in a ballet and a Broadway musical (neither very successful). In 1973 London's Royal Shakespeare Company received the Gillette play with spectacular success despite its dramatic shortcomings.

Naturally enough, a character so popular has found his way many times onto the screen. The productions have not always been outstanding, despite the gorgeous opportunities given by the foggy Victorian London backgrounds, but the involved murder yarns with their surprise denouements have kept their grip, and Holmes and his chronicler have been interpreted with success by a number of actors, one pair of whom, as we shall see, stood out above all others.

American Sherlock Holmes films are listed for 1903, 1905 and 1908. Between 1908 and 1910 there were a dozen Danish films starring Forrest Holger-Madsen; two German versions appeared in 1910. During the next few years a variety of Holmes films, all now lost, flooded in from every quarter, but the next outstanding actor to play the role was John Barrymore in 1922, and a negative of this film survives. Dr Watson was played by Roland Young, and the film succeeded as well as any silent film could when based on a character so given to witty conversation. In the same year in England a stage actor using the name Eille Norwood (apparently because he once knew a girl called Eille who lived in Norwood) made feature versions of *The Hound of the Baskervilles* and *The Sign of Four*. The latter at least still has its moments, with its climactic boat chase under Richmond Bridge. Hubert Willis was Watson, and the two actors repeated their roles in over forty two-reelers which came out in the next two years, most of them rather leaden-paced.

In 1929 Carlyle Blackwell played Holmes in an Anglo-German film of *The Hound of the Baskervilles* (much the most-filmed story). In the same year came the first sound film of the detective, *The Return of Sherlock Holmes*, with Clive Brook giving a good account of himself in a poor story. (The Americans simply could not leave the originals alone, and their tampering was seldom an improvement.)

More successful as a whole were five British films of the early thirties starring Arthur Wontner, a little old for the part but otherwise the second best Holmes ever seen on the screen. The films were cheaply but adequately made, and for the first time transmitted the authentic flavour of the stories, despite Ian Fleming's rather prissy Watson. The titles were *The Sleeping Cardinal*, *The Missing Rembrandt*, *The Sign of Four*, *The Triumph of Sherlock Holmes* and *Silver Blaze*.

1932 brought Raymond Massey as Holmes

Clive Brook, one of Britain's most distinguished actors, adopts a characteristic pose with magnifying glass for The Return of Sherlock Holmes.

and Athole Stewart as Watson in *The Speckled Band*, based on Conan Doyle's own play version of his story. Lyn Harding, who played the villainous Moriarty in several of the Wontner films, was equally villainous here as Dr Grimesby Roylott. In the same year, yet another *Hound of the Baskervilles* featured Robert Rendel; and Clive Brook appeared again in *Sherlock Holmes*, which confusingly was not based on the Gillette play but seemed to have a remote acquaintance with 'The Red-Headed League'. Reginald Owen, who played Watson, went on the following year to play Holmes in *A Study in Scarlet*, which borrowed nothing whatsoever from the Conan Doyle story of that name: but it gave Owen the distinction of being the only actor to play both roles.

Apart from a few German films, the later thirties were quiet for Holmes fans, as though in preparation for the appearance in 1939 of the greatest Holmes of all, Basil Rathbone. Curiously enough he was billed third in the cast list of *The Hound of the Baskervilles*, an affectionately remembered and reasonably faithful American

Here is Arthur Wontner in a portrait study from Silver Blaze: *the curved pipe and deerstalker are part of the essential paraphernalia.*

Even in 1921 Hollywood occasionally did location filming abroad. Here John Barrymore (in deerstalker) rehearses on the Thames Embankment.

version marred only by obvious studio moorland. Better was *The Adventures of Sherlock Holmes*, which immediately followed: here there was a loving Hollywood evocation of Baker Street and its environs (one only winced at fog in May). The screenplay owed something to Gillette, but not much. Despite a mysterious South American means of murder, a superbly incisive arch-villain Moriarty from George Zucco, and much chilling mumbo-jumbo about an albatross, the plot failed to hold water, and the final Tower of London scenes were rather silly, but no matter: the definitive Holmes and Watson were in command. Nigel Bruce played Watson as an endearing but gallant idiot, certainly a permissible reading; his wide-eyed incredulity and unswerving loyalty instantly seemed right. As Holmes, Rathbone was in total control: humorous, temperamental, gentlemanly, shrewd, brisk in action and a master of disguise (he even dressed up as a red-nosed comic and sang a music-hall song). If the plot made him too often too late in his deductions, well, that was the plot's fault. This film, by the way, can still be seen on ITV and gives rare delight.

Rathbone's Holmes was too good to lose. He performed it many times on radio, and between 1942 and 1946 he and Nigel Bruce made twelve further features in which, although the setting was updated for economy's sake to the 1940s, the plots, the deductions, the character-acting of most of the casts, and above all the relationship between the two bachelor heroes, were refreshingly according to Conan Doyle. These films are still highly popular on American television but have not been widely seen in the UK, though their time for reappraisal will undoubtedly come. The best of them include two faithful renditions, *Sherlock Holmes Faces Death* ('The Musgrave Ritual') and *The Pearl of Death* ('The Six Napoleons'); and two originals, *The Scarlet Claw* and *The House of Fear*.

Not till 1957 did Holmes appear on the screen again; then Peter Cushing played him rather fussily in yet another *Hound of the Baskervilles*, with André Morell a stalwart and sober Watson. Christopher Lee, Sir Henry in this film, later played Holmes in several German films which drew little approval from the

The most recent semi-serious incarnation of the great detective was in the person of Robert Stephens (standing) in Billy Wilder's The Private Life of Sherlock Holmes *which seems to have begun as a joke but develops into a rattling good yarn which would not have disgraced Conan Doyle. Colin Blakely, seated, is Watson.*

In 1971, nearly a hundred years after his creation, Holmes was still commanding such international renown that a satirical comedy, They Might Be Giants, *could be made about a psychiatric case who thinks he is Sherlock Holmes. George Scott is the gentleman; his doctor, played by Joanne Woodward, is naturally called Watson.*

Sherlock Holmes Society. In 1972 Stewart Granger appeared, with Bernard Fox as Watson, in a TV film version of *The Hound* which was hilarious for its carelessness: Baker Street was obviously a Parisian set done over, Baskerville Hall looked like a Mexican hacienda, and London was uniformly bathed in Californian sunshine. In these circumstances the actors could do little but look staunch.

Television series of Holmes have been unsatisfactory. Ronald Howard made twenty-six half-hour episodes in the early fifties, but apart from being cheap and nasty they had none of the required flavour. The BBC tackled the stories at length in the sixties, first with Douglas Wilmer and then with Peter Cushing, but the treatment was almost too faithful, showing that few of the stories could satisfactorily fill an hour: some seemed extraordinarily repetitive and tedious. Luckily, whatever films may be made in the

future, the original stories are still there to give pleasure for another hundred years and more. Ah, for the pleasure of reading for the first time such moments as the famous dialogue in 'Silver Blaze', when Holmes draws Watson's attention to 'the curious incident of the dog in the night-time'.

'But,' remonstrates Watson, 'the dog did nothing in the night-time.'

'That,' says Holmes sagely, 'was the curious incident.'

If you want to read the Sherlock Holmes stories, they are all (four novels and fifty-six stories) published by John Murray in various forms. If you are a real fan and can afford it, there is a marvellous two-volume set called The Annotated Sherlock Holmes, *full of pictures and footnotes of the time in which Holmes lived.*

DRAWINGS THAT WALK AND TALK

The History of Cartoons

We have already seen that a strip of movie film consists of a series of still pictures, each succeeding one showing the action at a slightly more advanced stage than its predecessor. In a live action film this succession of still pictures is obtained by photographing a moving scene with a cine-camera. If, however, each stage of the movement is hand-drawn on separate sheets of paper, and these drawings are then photographed one after another onto a single strip of film, an illusion of continuous movement will be produced when the film is run through a projector.

Animated cartoon films made in this way are almost as old as the cinema itself, and film-makers were quick to seize the opportunities they offered. The cartoon is the one type of film in which the film-maker can give free rein to his imagination, creating every possible and impossible type of man or animal and placing them in the most fantastic situations. The only drawback is the amount of work involved in producing even a short animated cartoon. Movie film is projected at the rate of twenty-four pictures every second, which means that a cartoon lasting for only one minute will require $24 \times 60 = 1440$ separate drawings. Because of this the characters and backgrounds in early cartoons were usually kept very simple.

The first really successful animated film was called *Gertie the Dinosaur*. Made in 1909 by an American artist named Winsor McCay, it was originally intended to be part of a live stage show. The film of Gertie was projected onto a screen on the stage and she appeared to respond to instructions given by McCay.

In about 1913 an artist called Earl Hurd came up with an idea that cut out a lot of the work involved in making a cartoon film. He drew the characters he was animating on sheets of clear celluloid. These cells, as they soon became known, were placed on top of a sheet of paper on which the background scene had been drawn and were then photographed, which meant that constant re-drawing of the background was no longer required. This method of making cartoon films has been used ever since.

Two other important pioneer cartoon-makers were Pat Sullivan, who created in Felix the Cat one of the first really popular cartoon characters, and Max Fleischer, who brought to the cinema screen the incredible adventures of the spinach-eating Popeye the Sailor.

But, of course, the best-known name of all, where cartoon films are concerned, must be that of Walt Disney. In 1923, in a converted garage belonging to his uncle in Los Angeles, and helped by his brother Roy Disney, he started to make a series of animated films. They were called *Alice in Cartoonland*, and contained a live girl, Alice, with drawn characters and background. He went

on to make a straightforward series of cartoons about a rabbit called Oswald, and then in 1928 on a train going from New York to Los Angeles he dreamed up the character that was to make him world-famous. Mortimer Mouse was the name he gave him, but before the train had reached Los Angeles, Walt Disney's wife had suggested 'Mickey' as a better name, and of course it was as Mickey Mouse that he became one of the most famous film stars of all.

Naturally, no one man could draw the vast number of pictures required for even a short cartoon, so cartoon studios like Disney's employ a small army of artists and technicians. The first stage in the production of a cartoon film is the 'storyboard'. For each scene in the film a rough drawing is produced. These are pinned up in sequence on a board, looking rather like a giant comic strip: they act as a plan and guide to all the various people involved. The most experienced artists known as animators then draw the important parts of the action, usually the beginning and end of a particular piece of movement. Their assistants follow this by drawing the in-between movements. Other workers, usually girls, next trace all their drawings onto clear plastic sheets, the cells we mentioned earlier. Finally the cells are painted in by yet another team of artists, again usually girls. Meanwhile other artists have drawn and painted the back-

The first stage in the making of an animated cartoon is the storyboard. It fulfils the same function as the script does in a normal live action film. This picture shows part of the storyboard for the Walt Disney feature cartoon Sleeping Beauty which was photographed in a wide screen process. Hence the wider than normal shape of the sketches.

ground scenery. The finished cells then go to the camera department where they are placed on top of the backgrounds and filmed.

It is in this latter stage of filming the completed cells that the Walt Disney Studios, in the mid 1930s, made a very important advance. Up to that time the various cells which go to make up a scene had simply been placed on top of one another, held down flat with a sheet of glass and then photographed. What the Disney Studios did was to devise the 'multiplane' camera. This consists of a metal structure about fifteen feet high. Built into it are a number of frames, one above the other, into which the various cells and backgrounds can be placed. Each frame can be moved separately, either up and down or across the structure. The camera is fastened to the very top with its lens pointing downwards. The multiplane camera is able to achieve an illusion of depth in this way, apparently moving through or across a scene, in the same way as an ordinary

A background artist at work painting the background scenes in front of which the characters on their transparent 'cells' will perform.

A Disney animator at work. Animators frequently make faces in a mirror to help them get the correct character expressions. The long sheet of paper on his right contains details of the exact timings and number of frames, or pictures, required for each bit of movement.

movie camera would, in photographing real-life scenes. For many years cartoon films were always quite short, seldom running for more than seven or eight minutes, but in 1934 Walt Disney started work on a film that was to change all that. It was *Snow White and the Seven Dwarfs* and as many as 750 artists worked on it in the years between 1934 and 1937, during which time they produced at least one million drawings. When it was completed in 1937 it ran for eighty-three minutes and was the world's first full-length animated feature film.

In the thirty years since *Gertie the Dinosaur* the cartoon film had certainly come a long way, and the years that have followed have seen a steady stream of full-length animated cartoon features from the Disney studios right up to their latest *Robin Hood*. Other studios and other animators of course have all contributed to the development and enormous popularity of cartoon films. In 1939 Max Fleischer, Popeye's creator, pro-

duced a full-length cartoon version of *Gulliver's Travels* and two years later followed it with another animated feature *Mr Bug Goes to Town* (English title: *Hoppity Goes to Town*). Most of the major Hollywood studios opened their own cartoon departments. From MGM came the violent but very funny Tom and Jerry. Warner Brothers had the wisecracking Bugs Bunny, followed by Sylvester and Tweety Pie. The first full-length British cartoon didn't reach the cinema screens until 1954, when the husband and wife team of John Halas and Joy Batchelor produced *Animal Farm*, a fairly adult fable based on a book by George Orwell.

Because the making of a cartoon film employs the talents and time of a great many people it becomes a very expensive business, so in recent years there have been attempts to simplify the whole process and break away, to a certain extent, from the very full and detailed style of animation pioneered and developed by the Disney Studios. In 1945 several of the leading Disney animators, including Stephen Bosustow and John Hubley, formed their own company UPA (United Productions of America). They produced a completely new style of cartoon film in

Tracing the animator's sketches onto the transparent plastic sheets known as 'cells'.

The Disney multiplane camera shown in operation. The camera itself is fixed to the top of the metal frame and shoots downwards through the various layers of paintings giving a feeling of depth and perspective to the scene.

which both the characters and background were kept extremely simple: sometimes they were little more than line drawings, highly imaginative and frequently very funny. Their characters included Gerald McBoing Boing and the short-sighted Mr Magoo. A Canadian animator, Norman McLaren, revolutionized the medium by actually drawing onto the celluloid itself, not only the visuals but the sound track, to create a very imaginative and effective form of cartoon. In Britain the leading exponents of this newer and highly individualistic style of animation have been Bob Godfrey, Richard Dunning and Richard Williams. You probably see their work most frequently in the form of television commercials, but Richard Williams is now completing, with a large team of animators, a full-length feature cartoon, his first. Based on an *Arabian Nights* story, its characters and backgrounds contain the sort of detail which we expect from a Disney cartoon, and hopefully it will meet with the success which Walt Disney's first feature cartoon *Snow White and the Seven Dwarfs* enjoyed. What is certain is that as long as the cinema exists, audiences will continue to enjoy 'drawings that walk and talk'.

The Richard Williams Animation Studios in London. Artists at work tracing and painting animators' drawings onto cells.

ABOVE *Scenes from Richard Williams' The Golden City. Still in production, this film promises to be one of the most exciting and original feature cartoons of recent years.*

BELOW *Richard Williams working on the character of 'Anwar', the evil grand vizier, and his vulture 'Brutay', who are featured in his new full-length cartoon* The Golden City. *Famous screen actor Vincent Price provides the voice of Anwar and the finished character sketches show a strong resemblance to Price himself.*

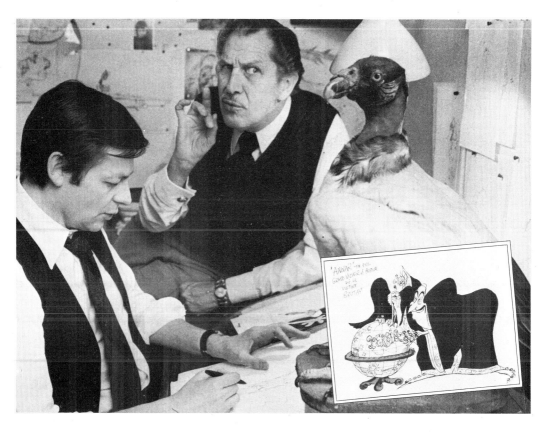

ABOVE *Scenes from Richard Williams' animated film version of Charles Dickens' Christmas Carol produced for American television. It won Richard Williams an Academy Award in 1972.*

BELOW **Snow White and the Seven Dwarfs:** *a landmark in the history of animated films. It proved that audiences would be prepared to spend an hour and a half watching a cartoon. Something that many critics doubted in 1937, when the film was released.*

OUR DEAR OLD FRIENDS

The Gentle Art of
Mr Laurel and Mr Hardy

Mr Laurel's appearance varied surprisingly through-out his career. The familiar grimaces and the shock of unruly hair (plainly a wig: see illustration on p. 33) made him instantly recognizable, but his actual features seemed to change from rounded to skeletal and back again, even in the same year.

Mr Hardy is at his most gentlemanly in this shot from a 1928 short called Early to Bed; *but pride goes before a fall, and Olly took some mighty falls in his time. For his considerable size he remained extremely agile, and never suffered the dire physical results one might expect from the punishment he took.*

In their heyday they were ignored or abused by the critics; now they have been the subject of several scholarly books and have achieved an eminence at least equal with Keaton and Chaplin in the history of comic cinema. A worldwide fan club thrives under the title 'Sons of the Desert', borrowed from one of their best films. If only they had known. The films of Laurel and Hardy, at least those whose negatives still hang coherently together, remain immensely popular on TV all over the world. It is sad that both Stan and Olly died before this belated recognition, and without receiving a penny of TV royalties.

Times were bad in the thirties, all over the world, and working-class people depended heavily on jokes. Especially in the north of England, it seemed that a good laugh would help to blow away all the hardships that unemployment brought, and there were cinemas that thrived, at fourpence a time, on showing nothing but comedies, presenting in effect a repertory of famous star comedians: Gracie Fields (yes, getting laughs then), Leslie Fuller, Leon Errol, Duggie Wakefield, Will Hay, George Formby, Frank Randle, Buster Keaton, Arthur Askey, Jack Hulbert, Ralph Lynn and Tom Walls, Wheeler and Wolsey and a score of others. We enjoyed them all, thoroughly. But our affection and love were reserved for one particular couple, two middle-aged, dark-suited, bowler-hatted fellows who strode regularly and cheerfully into our lives like visiting foolish uncles, accompanied by a silly tune called the cuckoo song. They made a few features, but were most often seen in shorts of two or three reels, shorts which were advertised in letters as big as the feature and which, after a run in the town centre, were fought for by all the suburban cinemas so that you could probably, as a regular cinema-goer, arrange to see each one five or six times if you liked. We remember that the ABC's publicity man once hit on a particularly happy turn of phrase. 'In addition,' the advertisement read, 'we have pleasure in presenting our dear old friends, Mr Laurel and Mr Hardy.' That was all. Not even the title of their latest adventure was given: it wasn't necessary. Stan and Olly were funny and sympathetic whatever they were doing, even if,

like members of the family, they were just being themselves. Nice, gentle, simple people were Stan and Olly, and it did us a power of good every month or so to renew our acquaintance with them.

Once you knew and loved their characteristics, there was no great element of surprise about their comedy routines. Their predictability, in fact, was what made them so funny, and that derived from the slow methodical pace of their gags, a style carried over from silent days with only a smattering of carefully devised dialogue and sound effects. Everyone except these two bumbling innocents could predict the exact outcome of any situation in which they were involved, because it would result directly from the kind of people they were. Olly's selfish pride, for instance, in preceding Stan through a doorway would promptly be followed by a painful fall, or at least a brick dropped on his head. Stan's childlike wonder and curiosity would inevitably land the pair of them in one fine mess after another. Whenever, as much married men, they decided to have a secret night on the tiles, their wives would find out about it and retribution would be speedy and cataclysmic. If, as happened occasionally, Stan did something impossibly, magically clever, such as lighting his pipe by flicking his thumb until it lit up in flames, Olly would diligently and

In this photograph from the early thirties, Stan and Olly are seen as themselves, looking much more intelligent but somehow less lovable than their familiar screen images. The man in the middle is producer Hal Roach, who brought them together.

Here are the boys as members of an orchestra in another 1928 film called You're Darn Tootin'. (Laurel and Hardy seemed to choose some of the most meaningless titles in film history, and even their most avid fans have difficulty in distinguishing between Hog Wild, Double Whoopee, Wrong Again, and We Faw Down, none of which seem especially relevant to the films they herald.) The film is climaxed by a street fight of which they are the innocent perpetrators, one of the most riotous scenes ever filmed.

crossly practise the feat until it worked wrong and he did himself an injury. These basic ideas never varied much, but they always came up fresh because variations were worked on them and because they were full of human truth.

Once seen, Stan and Olly could never be forgotten, for they were satisfyingly all of a piece. Stan (originally Arthur Jefferson, a Britisher from the Lake District) was short in stature and apparently in intellect, his long pale face animated from time to time by a curious set of expressions and gestures. There was the beaming self-satisfied smile from ear to ear; the claw-like scratching of the head accompanied by eyebrows raised in incomprehension; the myopic peer down the tilted nose for closer inspection of anything that wouldn't work or

was difficult to understand or had just been ruined by his own stupidity; the plain mouth pursed in indignation; the rare determined walk with swinging hips and flailing arms; the infantile tears. Olly, on the other hand, an American Southerner with a mellow voice, had a large physical presence (which made his agility on the run more remarkable) and was always dangerously sure of himself. His trademarks were his gallantry to ladies, his much-bruised but somehow untarnished dignity, his basic protection of the weaker Stan and his incurable optimism that their joint fortunes would change for the better. Till the better times come he will dust himself down after each catastrophe, and we know we shall continue to be privileged to see his 'I told you so' camera look and his embarrassed tie twiddle, and to hear his long sustained yell as disaster strikes off screen. Is there really less to savour in the adventures of this pair than in such acknowledged classics as Quixote or Boswell or Pickwick?

Typical of their interplay was the tit-for-tat routine which they brought to perfection and

This photo from Sons of the Desert (1933) shows Stan and Olly in their famous bowler hats or derbies, from which they were seldom separated; indeed they built many comedy sequences around them. The hats placed them somehow in suburbia, as foolishly respectable married men whose attempts to play tricks on their wives never succeed. Here they are trying (in vain) to persuade the ladies that they have just returned from Hawaii, whereas in fact they have spent a gay weekend in Chicago. Their sins will quickly find them out.

used time and time again: whole films were based on it. This was an exchange of physical violence, usually with a third party. It would start perhaps with a light unintentional blow, but grew rapidly in inventiveness and fury until the scene took on the appearance of a national disaster area. Features of the routine were the 'slow burns' which punctuated it. Each injured party, instead of exacting immediate retribution on his attacker, would fume quietly in close up before methodically preparing his next onslaught, while his opponent watched unflinchingly as the gluepot or the eggs were prepared, only wincing when the blow actually struck, and reacting only with a sigh to the camera. A brilliant example of this technique appears in one of the team's last and otherwise poorest films, *The Bullfighters* (1945). The boys are waiting for somebody in a Mexican hotel lobby dominated by a fountain with a circular seat around it. One man already sits here reading a paper, and Olly sits next to him with all his usual pomp and self-esteem, watching the world go by. Stan sits next to Olly but is quickly bored, and his fidgeting hand, which Olly cannot see, contacts a little tap, which he turns. A jet of water thereupon shoots out of the fountain and hits Olly in the back of the neck. By the time Olly has leaped two feet in the air and

For Bonnie Scotland *(1935) they abandoned the bowlers, finding that solar topees looked just as funny. Remembering what we said about their titles, you will not be surprised to learn that most of the film took place in India. And it may be the costumes, but doesn't Stan look fatter, and Olly thinner, than usual?*

In Swiss Miss *(1938) they wore Tyrolean costume but kept the bowler hats, which helped one to laugh at them before they actually did anything funny. The picture was not among their best, so every little helped; but it did contain the famous scene where they are carrying a piano across a rope bridge, and halfway across they meet a gorilla. (In Switzerland?)*

looked around to find the culprit, Stan, unaware of what has happened, is twiddling his thumbs innocently and looking the other way. Just at this moment the man with the paper chances to look up and gives Olly a pleasant smile. Olly eyes him uncertainly, looks at the camera for help which doesn't come, and finally decides to let the matter drop. He sits, and a half a minute later the process is repeated. This time Olly's fury knows no bounds; but being a gentleman, he is content to give a gentle reproof. He dips two fingers in the fountain water, shakes them almost dry, taps the newspaper reader's elbow and with a little smile and a shake of the head flicks the drops of water into his face. The man is astounded, but not to be got at in this way. He dips his hand in the water and flips the water at Olly without draining off a drop. Olly looks pained in close up for us, then grabs a handful of water and

After 1939 the Laurel and Hardy films declined in quality, through no fault of the stars, and by the time of Nothing But Trouble *(1945) they were making bricks with very little straw, and Stan was looking his age. You can bet that the pile of plates will be in smithereens by the end of the scene.*

hurls it. The man retaliates with two handfuls. Olly has a brainwave and fills his bowler... Very soon the whole foyer is flooded, the two protagonists are wringing wet, and Stan, the innocent cause of it all, continues to twiddle his thumbs and pretend he isn't involved. If Laurel and Hardy excelled at any one aspect of their craft, it was knowing how to milk a joke without tiring an audience.

Perhaps our favourite image of them is from *Way Out West* when they perform a soft shoe dance in the dust outside a saloon, and later, absurdly pleased with themselves, sing 'The Trail of the Lonesome Pine' at the bar counter.

From *Our Relations*, we cherish the moment when Olly decides they can afford only one glass of beer between them; he orders it, and Stan adds 'And two clean straws that haven't been used'. From *A Chump at Oxford*, when Olly as a butler expansively announces 'Come and get it folks, there's everything from soup to nuts', and Stan, impersonating a maid, is told, with entirely predictable results, to serve the salad undressed. From *Going Bye Bye*, the moment when Olly mistakes a can of condensed milk for the telephone receiver, and a moment later says in courtly tones: 'Pardon me for a moment, my ear is full of milk'. From *Them Thar Hills*, Stan's remark as he sits down to a repast of coffee and beans prepared by Olly: 'Boy, you sure know how to plan a meal'. From *County Hospital*, Stan's announcement to the invalid Olly: 'I brought you some hard-boiled eggs and some nuts'.

As a team, they made over fifty shorts and

twenty-three features. Stan worked hard on writing and producing most of them; Olly seems to have willingly done what he was told, remarking once: 'I have never really worked hard in the creation department'. Perhaps *Sons of the Desert* shows them at their most typical, as henpecked husbands who badly want to go to their Lodge's Chicago convention; so they hire a quack to say that Olly needs a sea cruise to Honolulu with Stan as chaperon. The boys have a whale of a time in Chicago, but fail to hear that the ship on which they are supposed to be has sunk, so their mourning wives are at the dock waiting for news when Stan and Olly, garlanded with flowers, arrive at their adjacent front doorsteps singing 'Honolulu Baby' to a small guitar. They discover the truth just as their wives return, and manage to hide in the roof. In the middle of the night the wives discover their presence and are out for blood. In pouring rain, the nightshirted boys are on the run over the roof and down a drainpipe. Stan descends first and lands in a huge overflowing water butt. Scrambling out, he calls up to his partner in crime: 'Olly, spread your legs'. So Olly does; and lands bottom first in the butt, with only his hands and feet visible above water. If this kind of thing does not strike you as funny, then the genius of Laurel and Hardy is not for you. Just to think of it makes us laugh till we hurt.

Most of the features are lumpy; some of the shorts are pure gold. In *Laughing Gravy*, a masterpiece of timing, they keep a dog in their room against landlord's orders, and find themselves out in the snow in their nightshirts. In *Towed in the Hole* they are fish merchants anxious to cut out the middle man; so they buy themselves a boat, paint it, and accidentally destroy it, all in one day. In *Big Business* they start out selling Christmas trees and goodwill to squint-eyed Jimmy Finlayson, and end up wrecking his house while he takes an axe to their car. Another orgy of planned destruction is *Helpmates*, in which Stan assists Olly to tidy up before the wife gets home. (When she gets home, there *is* no home.) In *Dirty Work* they are chimney sweeps. (Take it from there.) In *Hog Wild* they put a radio aerial on the roof. And they got an Academy Award for *The Music Box*, in which

Ironically, it was after their deaths that the greatest recognition and affection came to Laurel and Hardy. In the sixties several feature-length compilations were made from their funniest scenes, and met with a tremendous response even though the editing often interfered with their splendid timing. Now there is an international society, Sons of the Desert, devoted to spreading their glories, and in America they are almost the only subject of a monthly magazine called Pratfall. Three scholarly books have been devoted to them, and more are to come.

they spend three reels delivering a piano up a long flight of steps. Other enthusiasts plump for *Double Whoopee, Two Tars, The Battle of the Century, You're Darn Tootin', The Perfect Day, Come Clean, Going Bye Bye, Night Owls* or *Our Wife*.

Personally, we love 'em all.

If you want to read more about Laurel and Hardy, a good bookshop or library should be able to trace two excellent accounts of their work: Mr. Laurel and Mr. Hardy, by John McCabe (Museum Press 1961, later revised), and The Films of Laurel and Hardy (William K. Everson, Citadel Press 1967, later in paperback).

How 'Clapperboard' Get.

It is early evening on a Monday. You switch on your television—more probably, it is already on. Soon a familiar lively tune from *Mary Poppins*, 'Supercalifragilisticexpialidocious', heralds the start of another edition of 'Clapperboard'. As you settle back to enjoy the show (we hope) perhaps you sometimes wonder just how the programme reaches your screen.

The one you are watching will, in all probability, have started its life about four weeks previously, when it will have been little more than a rather vague idea. The themes of lots of 'Clapperboard' programmes are suggested by new films about to come into the cinemas, because one of the functions of 'Clapperboard' is to let you know about the new films in which we think you might be interested. Let us take such a programme as an example. We will suppose that a new John Wayne western is about to be released. John Wayne, of course, is one of the greatest cowboy stars and we may decide to make a programme all about the great cowboy stars of the cinema. The first thing to do, obviously, is to draw up a list of the stars we think should be included, but we have to bear in mind that it is only a twenty-five minute programme, so there isn't going to be time for more than about ten at the most.

To tell the story of the cowboy stars properly we ought to go back to the really early days of the movies, so we have to make sure that we include some of the silent western heroes such as William S. Hart and Tom Mix. And to bring the account really up to date we will include perhaps James Garner as well as John Wayne. Once the list has been decided, we next have to find the right films, but it may not always be possible to get hold of all the films we would really like. Sometimes, particularly in the case of old films, there may not be a print in the country. Then we have to substitute something else. Having eventually managed to borrow from the various film distributors prints of all the movies we want, they then have to be viewed for the selection of sequences. This is usually done on a special viewing machine, which allows the film to be run forwards or backwards, and even at three times normal speed, which of course helps to make the whole process much quicker.

In selecting sequences there are several points we try to bear in mind. Firstly each extract as far as possible should be a self-contained episode, so that a long explanation is not necessary for you to understand what is happening in the scene. It should reach some sort of climax at the end so that you are not left completely in the air wondering what happened. It should not be too long—about two and a half minutes is the usual length—and of course it should be entertaining and enjoyable for you to watch. There is a rather special problem we have to watch out for with more modern films which have been made for the wide screen. These films, projected in your local cinema, have a picture shape which is roughly twice as wide as it is high—the shape of a letter box—but your television set has a screen which is almost square. When a widescreen film is shown on television, therefore, only the centre part of the picture area can be seen and the outer edges have to be chopped off. When we are choosing an extract from such a film we have to make sure that it is a scene in which the main part of the action takes place round about the centre of the picture area, otherwise you might finish up with a picture of a blank wall and only the sound of the actors' voices coming from somewhere off screen, with perhaps just the tips of their noses showing at each side.

Once the various extracts have been selected, copies have to be made of them, because, understandably, the cutting up of expensive film prints is rather frowned upon. The next stage consists of assembling the bits of film containing the various sequences onto one large reel, in the order in which

Chris Kelly, in the Clapp[...] the programme.

The colour television cam[...] Kelly's head, but out [...] its boom.

rd studio, prepares to introduce

Also out of camera range is the television monitor set on which Chris can see the film clips.

s up the first shot. *Just above Chris* era range, is the microphone on

The director, in the centre, watches the various monitor screens in the control room. These enable him to preview pictures coming from the telecine machines and from the studio. The production assistant is on the right, and the vision mixer on the left.

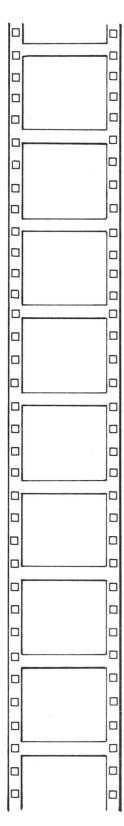

they will appear in the programme. If the extracts consist, as they often do, of a mixture of 35-mm film and 16-mm film, then, of course, they have to be made up into two reels, one for each gauge. With the films assembled, the script can be written. This consists of the words with which Chris Kelly will introduce and link each piece of film. Most important of all, the two components of the programme, films and script, have to be carefully and accurately timed to make sure they exactly equal the total running time which 'Clapperboard' is allowed. Timing is a vital factor in television, and every programme must begin and end within a few seconds of its exact scheduled time.

All is now ready for the final stage, the actual recording of the programme. This takes place in one of the large modern studios at Granada's Television Centre in Manchester. The film is loaded onto one or more of the telecine machines, which are really just the television version of a film projector. Chris Kelly faces the television cameras in the studio, while high above in the control room the director, production assistant and vision mixer sit at a long instrument-filled desk facing a battery of television screens. In the room next door are the sound engineers, and in another part of Television Centre an engineer stands ready to start the videotape machine on which the complete programme, picture and sound, will be recorded. In the studio itself, as well as Chris Kelly, are the cameramen and the floor manager, who receives his instructions through headphones from the director. All of the various technicians involved—the telecine operators, videotape engineer, sound recordists—are linked by intercom to the director and production assistant in the control room. Soon the time arrives, after a rehearsal, for the recording to commence. The production assistant gives the instruction 'roll VTR' and the videotape recorder starts running. It will be her job to keep a careful time check as the programme goes on, and tell the telecine operators when to start their machines. She must do this a few seconds before Chris stops talking because the telecine machines take a little time to get up to their correct speed. The director will, of course, control the whole operation, instructing the cameramen via their headphones and telling the vision mixer when to cut from one camera to another or from camera to film and back again.

So the recording proceeds until finally all the various film excerpts and Chris Kelly's linking pieces have been transferred onto the videotape, which a few days later will be played back onto your television set at home. And meanwhile, once a week, the planning of another programme begins...

Telecine control room. The word six which can be seen on one of the screens is part of a film 'leader' and shows that the film is ready to roll when the production assistant in the distant studio gives the word.

The Greatest Film Ever Made?

THE STORY OF 'CITIZEN KANE'

The kind of film you like best depends very much on your own personality. One person may adore Laurel and Hardy, German expressionist melodramas, and Katharine Hepburn; his best friend may be unable to stand them. Still, it is possible to stand back from one's own personal tastes and come to an objective judgment about a film's essential worth, significance, dramatic effectiveness, use of the medium and general professional competence. And whenever international critics have gathered together during the last thirty years to play the game of choosing the cornerstones of cinematic art, the film at the top of the top ten 'best films of all time' has almost invariably been *Citizen Kane*.

Clearly *Citizen Kane* is a film you should see if you intend to take any kind of keen interest in cinema and its history. It turns up on television every two years or so, but frankly it is best seen on a big screen, with an audience, so if your local film society isn't showing it, check with the National Film Theatre nearest you. See it, anyway; and here are some notes to help you understand and enjoy it.

Kane belongs to an age—the end of the thirties and the beginning of the forties—when Hollywood was at its peak of profitability, controlled by a handful of big studios, each buying up what talent it could and putting it under contract, usually squandering it in the process by forcing it through the mangle of commercial acceptability. Many of the world's greatest novelists and playwrights worked in Hollywood at this time, but you wouldn't know it from the resulting scripts, which bore their names but had

The thread of the film is a search for the meaning of Kane's dying word, 'Rosebud'. It turns out to be the name of the sledge he loved as a boy, the sledge which was taken from him when unexpected wealth sent him east for a grand education. Behind, Harry Shannon and Agnes Moorehead as Kane's parents; in the topper, George Coulouris as Kane's new guardian. Sonny Bupp as young Kane is showing the petulance which made Kane's adult life unhappy.

been revised and brought down by hacks to the lowest common denominator of the audience. Orson Welles was lucky: his contract stipulated that his first film at least should be revised by no one without his permission. This unheard-of condition was granted because Welles was the hottest of the day's 'hot properties'. Originally an actor, he had become a New York radio producer and had demonstrated his youthful genius so effectively that his radio version of H. G. Wells's *The War of the Worlds* literally panicked America: all over the country people who had tuned in halfway through the broadcast imagined that the Martians had really landed, and behaved accordingly. Orson Welles was headline news, and the studios outbid each other to implore him to come to Hollywood.

Kane (Orson Welles) marries his first wife (Ruth Warrick). This elaborate scene is on the screen for a brief moment only, and looks great; but the still lets you see that the fine building in the rear is a studio drawing. On the left you can just see where the backcloth meets the lawn.

RKO won, and Welles arrived in Hollywood with most of his repertory company of radio actors ('The Mercury Players'), to find a thick red carpet awaiting him. He could make whatever film he liked, at whatever expense (almost), and a studio full of technicians waited respectfully to hear his bidding. As he later remarked, it was 'the biggest toy train a boy ever had to play with'.

What film should he make? Welles considered and discarded thrillers, adventures and romantic dramas; finally he chose that most unlikely of all subjects for a commercial audience, political satire. He never admitted it at the time, but his project was fairly obviously a lampoon of millionaire newspaper publisher William Randolph Hearst, a genial but eccentric fellow who controlled his vast empire from a fairy tale castle he had built for himself on the California coast two hundred miles north of Hollywood. Welles was in fact more concerned with his personal life than his politics, with the personality of power and the inability of money to produce happiness. As the script developed, the parallels with Hearst's life became more marked: RKO officials swallowed hard, but Welles affected unconcern. (When the film was finished, Hearst tried to prevent it being shown, and his pet columnist Hedda Hopper railed at Welles in print; but RKO, with a surprising show of courage, ignored the threats, and the film, though no box office blockbuster, benefited from the publicity.)

Welles's collaborator on the script was an old Hollywood hand called Herman J. Mankiewicz, who died in 1953. To this day the argument continues as to who had most of *Kane*'s bright ideas. One suspects that Mankiewicz wrote the basic scipt and Welles tidied it up, though the whole affair is something of a mystery as nothing else in the career of either man has the tight-knit professionalism, depth of characterization or cinematic expertise of the *Kane* script, which still dazzles with its richness of phrasing and dramatic ideas. This is not to say that it is faultless; the final version leaves great unaccounted gaps in Kane's motivation, and the story is strung together on a rather pointless gimmick. But taken scene for scene, it was, and still is, a daring and magnificent feat of film-making.

The story runs as follows. Kane, a wealthy newspaper publisher but a failed politician and a disappointed man, dies alone and friendless at his great Florida castle, Xanadu. His last word is 'Rosebud'. A newsreel (then patterned after 'The March of Time'; today's equivalent would be TV's 'World in Action') is made about him, but the editor is dissatisfied because the facts offer little clue to Kane's real character. A reporter, Thompson, is sent out to interview all Kane's surviving friends and discover the meaning of 'Rosebud'. Kane's second wife

Kane buys up all the best talent from opposing newspapers and throws a party to celebrate the power of money. One of the most amusing scenes in the film, which, incidentally, was shot in deep focus, making objects equally clear whether they are in the foreground or the background.

had inadvertently been responsible for his political downfall; he had tried to set her up as an opera star but that too had failed. Unable to stand the old man's moods, she left him and is now an alcoholic cabaret artiste. Mr Bernstein, Kane's manager in his early days as a dynamic young newspaper publisher, gives a clue to Kane's childhood and the breakdown of his first marriage. Kane's college friend, Jedediah Leland, one-time dramatic critic for his paper,

Kane and his college friend Jedediah Leland (Joseph Cotten in his first film role) take over a newspaper and stand symbolically amid piles of their product. It is not clear why Kane should wear the jacket of a formal suit with old flannel trousers.

remembers how Kane in middle age lost his reforming ideas and was corrupted by power. His butler remembers the aged Kane and his terrible temper. And so on. No one finds out who Rosebud was; but as the film ends, and Kane's lifetime accumulation of expensive junk is being thrown into the furnace, the audience is allowed to see his childhood sledge, on which we have watched him play in the snow at the beginning of the film, go up in flames. On it is the word 'Rosebud'.

Many audiences, especially non-American ones, failed to recognize the sledge for what it was, and Welles has admitted that in any case it was a kind of throwaway irrelevancy, an anti-solution, for Kane to die remembering his childhood play rather than the more important things that happened in his life. What really matters is that the film is exciting from first to last, even though the solution to the 'mystery' is a let-down. It is superbly paced, with a brilliant, jazzy mocking musical score by Bernard Herrmann (who later wrote the music for Hitchcock's *Psycho*) which rockets one from scene to scene with tremendous brash confidence. The other main contributor is photographer Gregg Toland, who combined a grainy, contrasty look with a skilled use of deep focus, so that people a long way from the camera are as vivid as those in close-up. His

Kane returns from a European trip and receives a cup from his loyal staff. Note the care which has gone into engraving the cup, seen only briefly; the scene could easily have been shot in such a way as to make the engraving unnecessary, but Hollywood was always spendthrift in these matters. Note also Welles's insistence on the expensive habit of including the ceiling in this shot: dramatically very effective,

but time-consuming, and it makes the set difficult to light. Note also Kane's false nose. Welles has always felt that his own nose was too small for his face, and is seldom seen with the genuine article in view. The false ones in Kane *are generally quite becoming, but the different texture is perhaps more obvious in this shot. Holding the cup, Everett Sloane as Mr Bernstein.*

sense of composition, too, is brilliant throughout, so never allow yourself to see *Kane* on a modern wide screen, which will cut the top and bottom off the images; it was shot in a ratio of four by three, and must be seen that way.

Whatever the importance of the other contributors, including all the studio technicians, who were no doubt overjoyed to be working for once on a film that really used the medium, it was Welles who must have welded together all the parts and who therefore must receive responsibility for the success of the whole. What one remembers above all from *Kane* is its barrage of cinema tricks, which other directors had for years been too bored or idle to use: zooms, matt shots, zip pans, several conversations heard at one time, sentences begun in one scene and completed in another, cameras uptilted to show ceilings, silhouette shots, multiple mirror shots, crane shots, model shots, fast cutting, slow dissolves...the film is a technician's manual. All these tricks had been known before, but never had they been used in one film to such devastating effect.

Two scenes in particular stand out in the memory. The time-lapse breakfast table sequence is perhaps the most famous in screen history. After Kane's first marriage, he and his wife are seen at breakfast, one at each end of the table, both full of smiles and romantic thoughts. Then the camera pans back to him and he is older, too busy for her, tired after a night at the newspaper. It pans back to her and she is older again, slightly sulky and self-absorbed, starting their first quarrel. Another pan, and they are having a row about the care of their little boy. Finally, they are both middle-aged, not speaking at all, the long table separating them for ever. Ten years in the life of a marriage has been covered in two minutes.

The second brilliant sequence is the ten-minute newsreel at the start of the film. Apart from being an outstandingly accurate parody of 'The March of Time', it is a masterpiece of editing and special effects. Primitive newsreel material is mixed in with Kane's supposed career at that time, and the acted shots are grizzled and scratched to match the actuality, with jerky movement and cuts as might be expected. Kane as an old man is glimpsed at by a candid camera lurking behind a trellis while he takes his constitutional. Kane is seen with Hitler and other political figures, making absurd political prophecies. When it is over you can hardly believe that you have not been watching an account of a real life. Cleverest touch of all, later in the film many of the newsreel set-ups are repeated as seen by other eyes.

Welles seems to have enjoyed the rest of his career since *Kane*, which he made when he was only twenty-four, but professionally it has been somewhat of a decline. Although *Kane* did not lose money, Welles had shown his partiality for strange themes and his tendency to be a dangerous and expensive nuisance in a well-run studio, so the management had a go at recutting his next film, *The Magnificent Ambersons*, in his absence, and after a row his contract was terminated. He became a glowering romantic actor in films directed by others in his own style (*Jane Eyre*, *Journey Into Fear*) or in thinly scripted films directed by himself (*The Stranger*, *The Lady from Shanghai*). He became recklessly expensive and extravagant, to the point where no studio would employ him as a director. He came to Europe and between stage roles gave ham performances in some truly terrible films, always meanwhile amassing finance for projects

Kane in middle age is forced to sign away most of his fortune. A cleverly shot scene in which the vast space behind the desk accentuates Kane's loneliness and despair at a time of failure. At the time of filming, these three 'old men' were, from left to right, thirty-eight (Coulouris), twenty-four (Welles) and thirty-two (Sloane).

45

The ageing tycoon retreats to a massive palace called Xanadu, which he fills with the world's antiques. It makes a chill, dreary home for his young second wife, Susan (Dorothy Comingore), who spends her time doing jigsaw puzzles. Note the huge bellows and gigantic fireplace, which make her look smaller and lonelier.

of his own which took years to complete because he was seldom in the appointed place at the appointed time. Those which were finally completed made it difficult to believe that the same man had directed *Kane*: despite flashes of brilliance they had unforgivable lapses such as murky lighting and imperfect lip-synchronization. Clearly Welles had depended absolutely on the technical resources of the big studio; even though he had applied the touch of genius, his genius required control.

Rather oddly, the actors in his company fared better in Hollywood than he did himself. Joseph Cotten became one of the most famous romantic leads of the forties, and among those who carved substantial careers as character actors were Everett Sloane, Paul Stewart,

George Coulouris, Ruth Warrick and Ray Collins. But seldom did they shine so brightly as in *Kane*.

It must have been a series of incredible accidents that brought the supporting talents and the studio resources together with the full early flowering of Orson Welles during the summer of 1940, to make a young man's film about old age and to decorate it with a panoply of cinematic tricks. But they were accidents for which people who enjoy films will always be grateful. As long as films can be preserved *Citizen Kane* is likely to be counted among the most complex, significant and entertaining.

RIGHT *After Kane's death, the reporter (William Alland) and Kane's butler (Paul Stewart) survey the dismantling of the palace of Xanadu. They never discover the secret of Rosebud; only the audience, as the camera roves over the huge collection of art treasures, sees it being casually slung into the furnace. Incidentally, take a good look at the grey-suited pipe-smoking reporter in the centre of this still. It's Alan Ladd, big star of the forties; when* Kane *was made, he was still playing bit parts.*

ABOVE *Here is a long shot of the scene on the facing page. The vastness emphasizes the gulf between the Kanes. Can you see Mrs Kane, huddled beneath the giant fireplace? Those who have been lucky enough to visit the California home of real life millionaire W. R. Hearst, on whose life Kane is said to have been modelled, will see strong likenesses between this set of Xanadu and the real San Simeon.*

With the possible exception of Charles Chaplin, Walt Disney must be the most famous film-maker in the world. In his forty-three-year Hollywood career he won thirty-two Academy Awards and received countless awards from a host of nations. The cartoon characters which came from his studios have become better known than almost any human film stars.

Walt Disney (his full name was Walter Elias Disney) was born in Chicago in the United States on 5 December 1901. His father, Elias Disney, was an Irish Canadian and his mother Flora Call Disney was of German-American descent. Walt had three brothers and one sister. He spent his early life on a farm in Missouri and soon became interested in drawing, selling his first sketches to neighbours when he was only

---

RIGHT *Mickey talks: a scene from* Steamboat Willie (1928), *the first Mickey Mouse film to reach the cinemas and the world's very first 'talkie' cartoon.*

BELOW *The garage in Los Angeles which uncle Robert Disney allowed Walt and his brother Roy to use to make some of their first pictures.*

seven years old. The family returned to Chicago to live and Walt studied art at night school. After the First World War, during which he served as an ambulance driver in the Red Cross, he began his career as an advertising cartoonist in Kansas City. It was here that he managed to obtain a movie camera and made his first series of short animated cartoons. He called them 'Laugh-O-Grams' and sold them to a local cinema.

In August 1923 he left Kansas City for Hollywood with nothing but a few drawing materials, $40 in a well-worn suit and a short film, which he had just completed. Walt's brother, Roy, was already in California with $250. They pooled their resources, borrowed an additional $500 and set up a small animation studio in their uncle's garage. Soon they had completed their

ABOVE **Mickey's Fire Brigade:** *now featuring his friends Goofy and Donald Duck, this was one of the first Mickey Mouse cartoons to be made in Technicolor. Donald Duck's appearance was to change quite a lot from these early drawings.*

BELOW *The success of Mickey Mouse meant a move to new and bigger studios. When this photograph was taken in 1930 the brothers had already come a long way from uncle Robert's garage.*

ABOVE AND BELOW **Fantasia** (1940)
Mickey Mouse, Walt Disney's first star, played his greatest role as the Sorcerer's Apprentice.

BELOW AND RIGHT The dinosaurs from the 'Rite of Spring' sequence.

first film. It was called *Alice in Cartoonland* and it combined a 'live' Alice with drawn cartoon characters. It was a trick that the Disney studios were to use many times over the years right up to the recent *Bedknobs and Broomsticks* in which David Tomlinson refereed a football match between two teams of cartoon animals. *Alice in Cartoonland* was successful, and a New York film distributor gave them an order for a whole series of cartoons. Soon the brothers were able to expand into larger premises and Walt was joined by an old friend from his Kansas City days, a brilliant artist and animator with the unlikely name of Ub Iwerks.

The next Disney character to appear was a rabbit named Oswald, and then in 1927 came Mickey Mouse. We have already described how Walt got the idea for Mickey on a train journey from New York to Los Angeles. The first Mickey Mouse cartoon, *Plane Crazy*, which was drawn mainly by Ub Iwerks, also introduced Mickey's lifelong leading lady Minnie Mouse. The enthusiasm with which Walt's small staff completed the cartoon faded when no distributor

wanted to buy the film, on the grounds that women are scared of mice! Refusing to give in, they started production on another Mickey Mouse cartoon, *Galloping Gaucho*. But before it was finished Warner Brothers released *The Jazz Singer* with Al Jolson and ushered in the era of talkies. Both the Mickey Mouse cartoons had, of course, been silent pictures, and Walt was quick to realize the enormous advantage sound could give to cartoons. He immediately started work on a third Mickey Mouse cartoon, *Steamboat Willie*, this time in sound.

On 29 October 1928, at the Colony Theatre in New York, Mickey Mouse made his debut in *Steamboat Willie*, the very first talkie cartoon, and scored an overwhelming success. Mickey Mouse became a major star overnight and enabled Walt Disney to go ahead with a whole series of short cartoons. Such was Mickey Mouse's popularity with movie audiences that soon cinemas were displaying posters that read 'Mickey Mouse Playing Today!' Walt himself did Mickey's voice for many years, and during the 1930s he produced ninety Mickey Mouse cartoons in which

ABOVE *Bacchus from Beethoven's Pastoral Symphony (Fantasia).* BELOW *Arabian Dance, from Nutcracker Suite (Fantasia).*

BELOW *Artist's character sketches for the ostrich dancers who perform the 'Dance of the Hours'.*

OSTRICH DANCERS
DANCE OF THE HOURS
CONCERT
FEATURE
·F-128·

51

ABOVE **Snow White and the Seven Dwarfs** (1937): the first ever full-length cartoon and one of the most successful films the cinema has ever seen. Its immediate popularity with audiences ensured the continued growth and progress of the Disney studios.

The immortal Bambi first came to the cinema screens in 1942.

Mickey played everything from a fireman to a giant killer, from a cowboy to an inventor, from a detective to a plumber. As well as Minnie, he was eventually joined by a whole family of animated characters, Clarabelle Cow, Horace Horsecollar, Goofy, Pluto, Peg-leg Pete and, of course, the bad-tempered Donald Duck.

With the success of Mickey Mouse cartoons well established, the Disney studios started work on a new series of more artistic, unrelated cartoons, the *Silly Symphonies*. Technicolor was introduced for these in 1932 and Walt Disney won his first Academy Award for one of them, *Flowers and Trees*. Two years later, in 1934, he began production of his greatest project up to then, the world's first full-length cartoon feature: *Snow White and the Seven Dwarfs*. It took almost three years to complete and had its world

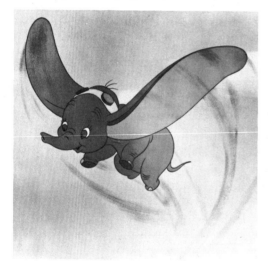

ABOVE AND BELOW *Dumbo*, the delightful flying elephant, was the fourth Disney full-length cartoon and first appeared in 1941.

The Jungle Book (1967): Walt Disney's cartoon version of Rudyard Kipling's famous story. One of the film's high spots was Phil Harris singing (as the voice of Baloo the bear) of 'The Bare Necessities'. It was the last animated feature to be personally supervised by Walt Disney.

première in Los Angeles on 21 December 1937. It had cost two million dollars to produce, but fortunately for Walt Disney and his studio it was an immediate success with audiences throughout the world, and of course it has continued to give enormous pleasure to generations of moviegoers ever since. It earned for Walt Disney a special Oscar at the 1939 Academy Award ceremonies. Nine-year-old Shirley Temple presented him with the award which was inscribed 'To Walt Disney for *Snow White and the Seven Dwarfs*, recognized as a significant screen innovation which has charmed millions and pioneered a great new entertainment field for the motion picture cartoon'.

The success of *Snow White* encouraged Disney to start work immediately on two more feature-length cartoons. The first, *Pinocchio*, was based on a popular nineteenth century folk tale by Carlo Collodi. For the cartoon version of the story of Pinocchio, the little wooden puppet who comes to life, Walt Disney created a new character in Jiminy Cricket, a chirpy little fellow who acted as Pinocchio's conscience. He offered the puppet guidance and advice in the form of two songs, 'Give A Little Whistle' and 'When You Wish Upon A Star'. Both songs became smash hits and 'When You Wish Upon A Star'

Over the years Walt Disney and his artists and technicians have won numerous awards and he is pictured here with many of them. They number about five hundred major awards including thirty Oscars from the Academy of Motion Pictures Arts and Sciences.

Walt Disney sits in on a story conference during an early and vital phase in the development of the 1951 feature cartoon Alice in Wonderland.

Watching the pictures on the studio theatre screen, technicians put the finishing touches to the soundtrack of The Sword in the Stone. *The mass of switches and knobs on the control panel in front of them enables them to mix and blend the various separate sound tracks into the one final track.*

Robert Newton in his most memorable role as the rascally Long John Silver in the first Walt Disney live action feature Treasure Island, *made in Britain in 1950.*

A scene from the 1963 full-length cartoon The Sword in the Stone.

is virtually the signature tune of the Disney Studios.

Pinocchio reached the cinemas in 1940, the same year as Walt Disney's third feature cartoon *Fantasia*. In its time *Fantasia* was a daring and unique experiment. Instead of telling a straightforward story, as the two previous feature cartoons had done, it set out to interpret visually some of the world's finest music. One of its most famous sequences featured Walt Disney's old friend Mickey Mouse as 'The Sorcerer's Apprentice', vainly battling with legions of pail-carrying brooms; another sequence based on Bach was totally abstract.

Between 1937 and 1966 Disney *personally* produced sixteen full-length cartoons. As well as the three we have mentioned they include *Dumbo* (1941), *Bambi* (1942), *Cinderella* (1950), *Alice in Wonderland* (1951), *Peter Pan* (1953), *Lady and the Tramp* (1955), *Sleeping Beauty* (1959), *101 Dalmatians* (1961), *The Sword in the Stone* (1963), and *Jungle Book* (released 1967).

In 1947 the Disney Studios broke away, for the first time, from cartoon films, when they made the first 'True Life Adventure', *Seal Island*, which of course featured real animals instead of animated ones. For several years, in fact, Disney

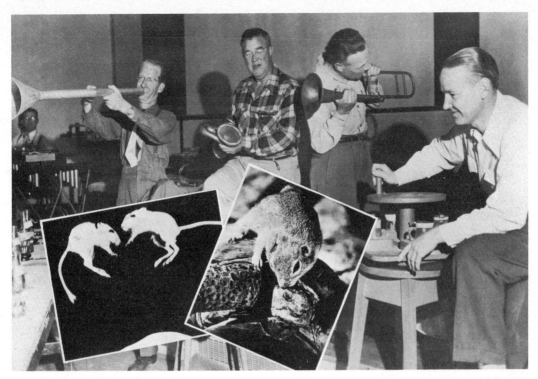

ABOVE *The True Life Adventures marked a new departure for the Disney studios in 1949. Here is the sound department recording the 'Symphony of the Mud Pots' from* The Living Desert *(1953).*

BELOW *The True Life Adventures have been distinguished by remarkable wildlife photography like this scene of two prairie dogs getting into a skirmish from* The Vanishing Prairie.

ABOVE *The latest Disney venture: Disneyworld in Florida. An aerial view of the Magic Kingdom Park. In the far background the castle; centre the railway station and in the foreground the riverboat.*

BELOW *The Mad Hatter's Tea Party ride in Disneyland, California.*

The magnificent Cinderella Castle, at 180 feet, the tallest structure at Disneyworld.

cameramen had been filming real animals to act as a guide to the cartoon animators and it seemed an obvious step to extend this filming and produce a series of wildlife pictures. At first these were short films and then in 1953 came the first full-length True Life Adventure *The Living Desert*. A fascinating film, it showed that the desert is not a dead desolate place as you might suppose, but is filled with a wide variety of plant and animal life.

Alongside the True Life Adventures came a series of live action feature films, which started with a version of Robert Louis Stevenson's classic adventure story *Treasure Island*, produced in England in 1950. It starred Robert Newton in what is certainly his best-remembered role as the rascally but very likeable Long John Silver.

Amongst the live action films to have come from Walt Disney since then have been *Robin Hood* (1952), *Twenty Thousand Leagues Under the Sea* (1955), *The Swiss Family Robinson* (1960), and of course the magical *Mary Poppins* (1964).

In the last ten years or so of his life Walt Disney devoted a great deal of his time to designing and building his pet projects of Disneyland and Disneyworld, funfairs extraordinary. He died on 15 December 1966, already a legend. He brought enormous pleasure and happiness to generations of children and adults throughout the world, and will certainly continue to do so as long as his films are shown.

57

ROBIN HOOD

The most recent full-length cartoon to come from Walt Disney Productions is Robin Hood, and in making it they have given a new twist to the familiar and popular legend. In the words of the film's producer–director Wolfgang Reitherman, this new version of Robin Hood is told 'as seen through the eyes of the animals of Sherwood Forest who knew Robin best'. Hence all the characters are played by animals.

In a cartoon feature like Robin Hood the voices of the characters are almost as important as the drawings themselves. In many cases the actors who will provide the voices are chosen before the final details of the cartoon characters are worked out. Because of this, quite often characteristics of the human actors creep into their cartoon counterparts.

Robin Hood is a crafty adventurous Fox whose voice is that of British actor Brian Bedford.

The voice of Sir Hiss, Prince John's snake counsellor, is provided by Terry Thomas. His bristling moustache, familiar gap between his front teeth and pompous air are cleverly captured in his cartoon counterpart.

Singer and composer Roger Miller provides the voice of the minstrel rooster Alan-a-Dale, who recounts the Robin Hood story in the film.

When Prince John organizes an archery contest in the hope of trapping Robin, the wily fox turns up heavily disguised as a stork.

Robin's faithful companion Little John is a fun-loving bear with the voice of Phil Harris. Amongst the previous voices he has supplied for Disney cartoons were those of Baloo in The Jungle Book and O'Mally in The Aristocats.

The story's romantic interest is of course supplied by Maid Marion, a vixen whose voice is provided by English actress Monica Evans. This scene is a good example of the illusion of depth which can be created with the Disney multiplane camera.

Peter Ustinov is the voice of Prince John, a scrawny thumb-sucking lion.

Friar Tuck, here putting the squeeze on Sir Hiss, is a badger with the voice of veteran character actor Andy Devine.

THEY TURNED
THE TIDE AT
ANZIO!!!

JAMES
DRURY
Star of
"THE VIRGINIAN"
TV SERIES

THE YOUNG
WARRIORS

TECHNICOLOR®
PANAVISION®
co-starring
STEVE CARLSON · ROBERT PINE
JONATHAN DALY

Young people who find they have an interest in the art and craft of film, and especially in the historical aspects, used to have a hard time of it. Only the most popular films were reissued, and that is not always to say the best. Negatives were seldom well looked after, and even the film-makers themselves, in the rare cases where they had control, were not the best judges of what in their own work should be preserved. (There is a grim 1937 story of Frank Capra personally hurling into a furnace the first three reels of negative of the original *Lost Horizon*, because he thought they seemed slow; thirty-five years later, film buffs around the world would give their eye teeth to see them.) The growth of the Classic cinemas and a few 'specialized halls' in university towns did something to help, but the choice of revivals was very erratic. The British Film Institute began its activities in 1934 and the National Film Archive came shortly after, but opportunities to see the films preserved were few: unless a spare 'projection print' was obtained, the material was reserved for posterity. Not till the Telekinema, later the National Film Theatre, was built on London's South Bank in 1951 was there available to the British public at large a regular repertory of the world's most

---

The Young Warriors? *It's an unknown film, having barely been released to cinemas in Britain, but the star is James Drury, who was liked in* The Virginian. *So that's something for the women; the war theme will please men; and it's a good title. OK for peak time.*

interesting films. Even then, one had to be a member, and the number of people who could regularly visit the South Bank was of course quite small.

Television changed all that. The main purpose of the new medium was to make its own kind of programme and create its own kind of art, but feature films were obviously an attractive ready-made alternative to the main product: a good one would lend great variety and interest to an evening's programme. Unfortunately, the film industry did not see things that way. Cinema-owners and film-makers thought of television as a one-eyed monster that threatened to take away their audience. It did just that, of course, but it was going to anyway, so spitting in its eye was rather silly. But spit the movie-men did, and in America the contest became really fierce. In Britain the film industry slowly

Disney's Pinocchio *? Marvellous if you could get it. But the Disney organization has a strict policy about its feature cartoons, not to let TV have them while they can still be successfully reissued to cinemas. And as they provide fresh and unfading delight for succeeding generations of children, you won't be seeing* Snow White *or* Dumbo *or* Fantasia *on your sets for a very long time.*

ABOVE **When Worlds Collide** *? Men like science fiction better than women, so it's thought best not to play this kind of thing during the week, when the ladies usually control the switch. Early on Saturday evening, or on Sunday afternoon, it should please the majority.*

The whole world loves Tom Jones!

Tom Jones? *One would have thought so: in cinemas it was one of the most successful films of the sixties. But perhaps people remembered it too well, for on TV it was not particularly popular...*

banded together to find ways of preventing films being sold to television, mainly at first by threats of blackballing any member who did sell. Producer Danny Angel, for instance, sold his few films to TV and was prevented from working in the industry again. Then the Film Industry Defence Organization—FIDO for short—was set up as a kind of watchdog which also, by imposing a small levy on every cinema admission, could accumulate enough funds to pay independent producers *not* to put their films on television. (The big corporations were supposed to hold back without subsidy for the good of the industry.) Thus many second feature producers were able to get large sums of money for not offering for sale downright awful films which television would not have touched with a bargepole anyway. A very few good ones were to be found among the FIDO purchases, and, unluckily, although FIDO is no longer active as a buyer, such films as Carol Reed's *Kipps* and

Night Train to Munich, which would make delightful TV entertainment, are locked in the vaults for years to come.

What finally drew FIDO's teeth was a back door sale of many valuable film libraries. RKO, for instance, shut up shop and its films passed into hands outside the industry, who could not be prevented from selling to whom they pleased. Then several of the major corporations found moral loopholes. They had promised they would not sell their own films to television, but supposing they acquired each other's? By a complicated series of manoeuvres the pre-1948 American films gradually changed hands, so that Paramount's were in the control of Universal, Warners' went to United Artists, and Warners themselves were poised to sell the Fox library. FIDO could think of no objection

---

Humphrey Bogart? *Well, the forty-eight films are not all of high quality, and a few are comedies and musicals, so they can hardly be called 'action-packed'. But Bogart is the most durable of stars, still commanding attention nearly twenty years after his death. So yes to the good Bogart films, but late at night, because they have all been shown rather often in peak time.*

48 ACTION-PACKED FEATURES WITH SHATTERING IMPACT!

ACROSS THE PACIFIC · ACTION IN THE NORTH ATLANTIC
ALL THROUGH THE NIGHT · AMAZING DR. CLITTERHOUSE
ANGELS WITH DIRTY FACES
BATTLING BELLHOP (KID GALAHAD) · BIG CITY BLUES
THE BIG SHOT · THE BIG SLEEP · BLACK LEGION
BROTHER ORCHID · BULLETS OR BALLOTS · CASABLANCA
CHAIN LIGHTNING · CHINA CLIPPER · CONFLICT
CRIME SCHOOL · DARK PASSAGE · DARK VICTORY
THE GREAT O'MALLEY · HIGH SIERRA · INVISIBLE STRIPES
ISLE OF FURY · IT ALL CAME TRUE · KEY LARGO
KING OF THE UNDERWORLD · MALTESE FALCON
MARKED WOMAN · MEN ARE SUCH FOOLS · OKLAHOMA KID
ONE FATAL HOUR · PASSAGE TO MARSEILLE
PETRIFIED FOREST · RACKET BUSTERS
RETURN OF DOCTOR X · THE ROARING TWENTIES
SAN QUENTIN · SWING YOUR LADY
THANK YOUR LUCKY STARS · THEY DRIVE BY NIGHT
THREE ON A MATCH · TO HAVE OR HAVE NOT
TREASURE OF SIERRA MADRE · THE TWO MRS. CARROLLS
VIRGINIA CITY · WAGONS ROLL AT NIGHT
YOU CAN'T GET AWAY WITH MURDER · BAREFOOT CONTESSA

to that. It all sounds rather foolish, and it was. But what caused the floodgates finally to open, in 1964, was the decision of movie mogul Samuel Goldwyn, in his eighties, that he would make no more movies and was ready to sell to television fifty of his best. He did, to ITV; and all his rivals suddenly gave up and indulged in an undignified scramble to unload as many films as possible onto a surprised market.

Oddly enough, the Goldwyn films were not especially popular on British television, apart from a few classics such as *Wuthering Heights* and *The Little Foxes*. The Danny Kaye musical comedies were particularly disappointing. But the damage was done. Both BBC and ITV were able to take their pick of the film libraries, at fairly modest prices, the industry's only proviso being that no film should be shown until five

Zanzibar? *Well, it looks great, but in fact this is a thirty-year-old black and white potboiler, very cheaply made and by no means presenting the spectacle suggested except in the form of clips stolen from even older films. As the stars have also faded, the film does not seem worth reviving: the same kind of adventure is much better done these days, on real locations.*

Perfect Strangers? *A rather old romance aimed at women. Nothing wrong with that, but the stars no longer have much draw, and the title could be confused with a British film of the same name. So probably not.*

years after its original release date. At that time only two or three films a week were being shown on each channel, so there were plenty of films to go round; but in more recent years BBC 2 has come in, and the restrictions on transmission hours have gradually been removed, with the effect that in any one week ITV is usually showing ten or eleven features (including those made specially for television, of which more later) and the two BBC channels about twelve between them. Even allowing for some of these being repeats, it is obvious that the demand is now much greater than film-makers, in these days of dwindling production, can supply. So good films are bought up for TV almost as soon as they are released, even though they are not available for five years, and the good ones are in such demand that the industry has been able to raise its prices to a point where films may become too expensive to buy. Another problem is that many of the films made in the last few years are simply too violent, too horrific, or too adult in other ways to be acceptable on the living room set in the average home. One could probably show them without complaint late at night, but few people watch at that time and economics would prevent films being bought at high prices for a very small audience.

This problem arose first for American television, where each station shows dozens of films a week. (American audiences have been exposed to the worst second features ever made, whereas in Britain we have on the whole restricted our purchases to films which played top of the bill.) The answer was to make films specially for television. At first it seemed that this could not be done with the money available, but serious thought made all concerned realize that what makes filming so expensive is the ambition of writers and directors to achieve 'perfection' by making up to fifty shots of each scene if necessary, and by the cost of talent. TV movies were finally made by restricting stories mostly to interiors or at any rate by excluding expensive action sequences; by ignoring high-priced fashionable actors and directors and turning instead to some of the popular stars of ten or twenty years ago (which is when the TV audience was going to cinemas anyway), now idling away their lives on what remains of their big incomes; and by keeping production values down to a modest limit. The first season of these seventy-three minute movies was not encouraging; they seemed like one-hour series episodes unnaturally drawn out, with obvious pauses every five minutes for commercials. But practice made perfect; the second year brought competent series like 'Mystery Movie' and by year three well-known stars were falling over themselves to get into TV films like *Haunts of*

Gone With the Wind? *Yes, grab it. But we can't. This 1939 epic seems to have magical powers: every three or four years they reissue it and it brings in yet another stack of money. Our guess is that it will be the last old film to be released to TV...and we may have to wait another five years for a chance to buy it. (Did Vivien Leigh really look so young in 1939? And wasn't Clark Gable perfect as Rhett Butler?)*

The Silver Chalice? *A very long film from a very long novel not remembered here. Semi-biblical films are no longer very popular, but if one can find a slot that length it will get by on the strength of Paul Newman, though this was his first film and frankly he wasn't very good in it, as he freely admits.*

the Very Rich, A Cold Night's Death and The Alpha Caper.

Viewers often write to ask, why can't you show Gone With the Wind, or The Wizard of Oz, or Doctor Zhivago? The answer is that while a film can still be profitably revived in cinemas it will not be sold to free television. A television buyer's resources are limited, and he can never afford to pay the kind of price that a successful nationwide reissue would bring. A film like The Wizard of Oz, for instance, has been making money for more than thirty years, cropping up all over the country during every school holiday. One tries not to buy rubbish, but then one man's rubbish is another man's antique. Over the last two years Granada has been scheduling, to the great delight of many viewers, forty-year-old Charlie Chan and Mr Moto mysteries, and jolly good of their kind they are; but you will still find people writing letters demanding something newer and in colour (even if its entertainment value is less). You can't please everyone all the time; and very boring life would be if you could.

The Eddie Cantor Story? *A well-produced film, but Cantor is an entertainer scarcely remembered in this country, and this is not really himself in action, but an impersonation by Keefe Brasselle. (Who?) Even when new it did not have anything like the success of* The Jolson Story, *which seemed better in every way. So no, leave it on the shelf.*

Film in all Sizes

Various film sizes (or gauges) have been used throughout the history of the cinema, and they are always referred to by their width in millimetres. The principal one, however, used from the cinema's earliest days, is thirty-five millimetres wide. This is the size used in most professional cinemas today. It is also widely used for showing feature films on television.

Cameras and projectors for 35-mm film are generally rather bulky and heavy, so just after the First World War smaller film sizes were introduced to cater for the then new hobby of amateur film-making. In 1922 the French Pathé Company introduced 9·5-mm film, together with cameras and projectors to use it. This remained the most popular size of film for amateur use, in Europe, until after the Second World War, and is still used by a minority of enthusiasts. Early in 1923 the Kodak Company in America brought out their 16-mm film. Originally intended like 9·5-mm for amateurs, this size is now mainly used by professionals, particularly in television. In recent years a number of feature films have been made in this size and then enlarged onto 35-mm film for theatre presentation. Many of the Walt Disney True Life Adventures were made in this way, the smaller and lighter 16-mm cameras being ideally suited to wildlife photography. In 1933 Kodak introduced, for amateur use, 8-mm film, which they obtained by simply slitting 16-mm film in half. This size, together with its more recent version, super 8-mm is the size used for most home movies throughout the world.

At various times other sizes such as 28-mm and 17·5-mm (made by slitting standard 35-mm in half) have appeared and as quickly disappeared. 70-mm is occasionally used today for giant screen presentations in some specially equipped cinemas. The special equipment has to include a hoist to lift the huge reels of film onto the projector.

35-mm
Showing the soundtrack running down the edge of the picture area.

16-mm
When a soundtrack is added the film is perforated on one side only to leave room for the track.

9·5-mm
The central perforation allowed the maximum amount of film area to be used for the picture.

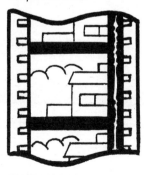

The perforations in Super 8-mm were reduced to half the size of those in ordinary 8-mm film, which gave a fifty per cent increase in picture area.

8-mm

Super 8-mm

DON'T ALWAYS BELIEVE
WHAT YOU READ IN THE PAPERS
A Selection of Misleading Movie Advertisements

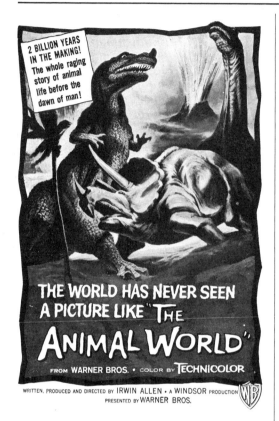

Since the beginning of movies it has been the fashion to advertise them in superlatives, as though each one that came along was the greatest thing that ever happened. Here are a few amusing examples, to be taken with a large pinch of salt.

ABOVE **The Animal World** The claim '2 billion years in the making' is too outrageous to be anything but funny, and must have been so meant. Students of prehistory will probably tell us in any case that it was not two billion years ago that dinosaurs walked the earth.

ABOVE RIGHT **International Lady** 'A thousand thrills ..' Did anyone count them? In fact one would be very lucky to get more than a dozen exciting moments in any film.

RIGHT **The Rising of the Moon** If John Ford ever uttered the words quoted here, they don't appear in the files on him. Certainly the film was a very rushed job, and no critic in the world would place it among his best. Note that the excellent principal actors from Dublin's Abbey Theatre are not credited by name, whereas a star like Tyrone Power is given big billing for adding a few words of introduction.

LEFT **Genghis Khan** 'In the eight centuries...no man has matched the magnificence of his adventure.' Can they prove that? No.

ABOVE **Robinson Crusoe on Mars** 'This film is scientifically authentic...' To be so, presumably, it would have to be shot on Mars. In fact it was photographed in Death Valley, California.

BELOW **Satellite in the Sky** 'Today the world's most guarded secret will be revealed.' It sounds like a newspaper story, but in fact is meant to refer to the fiction on which the film is based.

THE MOST EXPLOSIVE STORY OF OUR TIME!

FAIL SAFE

COLUMBIA PICTURES presents A MAX E. YOUNGSTEIN Sidney LUMET production

FAIL SAFE

starring DAN O'HERLIHY · WALTER MATTHAU · FRANK OVERTON
EDWARD BINNS · LARRY HAGMAN and introducing FRITZ WEAVER

also starring HENRY FONDA as The President

Screenplay by WALTER BERNSTEIN · Based on the best-selling novel by EUGENE BURDICK & HARVEY WHEELER · Produced by MAX E. YOUNGSTEIN · Directed by SIDNEY LUMET

LEFT **Fail Safe** *The ad suggests spectacular scenes of destruction. In fact the film leads up to the inevitability of such destruction, but the scenes are never shown.*

BELOW **In the Foreign Legion** *and* **Meet the Mummy** *How can two Abbott and Costello films both be 'their funniest by far'?*

RIGHT **Captain Blood** *There are ads for this film describing Errol Flynn as 'six feet four of fighting British manhood' (he was actually at least four inches less, and Tasmanian), but we like this one promising 'giant galleons blown to bits'. The studios did have a full-size galleon at the time, but what was blown to bits was an 18-inch model.*

THEIR FUNNIEST-BY-FAR LAUGHS-FOR-ALL HIT!

They risk the curse of Old King Tut when they get chummy with the mummy in the crypt!

UNIVERSAL PRESENTS

BUD ABBOTT and LOU COSTELLO MEET The Mummy

with MARIE WINDSOR · MICHAEL ANSARA and PEGGY KING singing "You Came A Long Way From St. Louis"

Directed by CHARLES LAMONT · Screenplay by JOHN GRANT · Produced by HOWARD CHRISTIE

THEIR NEWEST and FUNNIEST BY FAR! and their FIRST in a YEAR!

They join the Foreign Legion and burn up the burning sands...with HILARITY!

UNIVERSAL PRESENTS

BUD ABBOTT and LOU COSTELLO in The FOREIGN LEGION

with PATRICIA MEDINA *That sly spy from "FRANCIS"*

WALTER SLEZAK · DOUGLASS DUMBRILLE

Screenplay by JOHN GRANT, MARTIN RAGAWAY and LEONARD STERN
Directed by CHARLES LAMONT · Produced by ROBERT ARTHUR

PRINCE TURNED PIRATE
TO FIGHT THE KING'S ARMADA
AND WIN A WOMAN'S KISS!

ERROL FLYNN
and
OLIVIA de HAVILLAND
together!

HIS SWORD CARVED HIS NAME ACROSS THE CONTINENTS —AND HIS GLORY ACROSS THE SEAS!

Giant galleons blown to bits and sent to the bottom!

RAFAEL SABATINI'S
"Captain Blood"
A WARNER BROS. RE-RELEASE

WITH
BASIL RATHBONE · GUY KIBBEE · HENRY STEPHENSON · ROBERT BARRAT DIRECTED BY MICHAEL CURTIZ

ABOVE **Woman in White** 'Its every scene is on the screen.' A flagrant lie! Wilkie Collin's Victorian mystery is enormously long and complex: the 1947 film is a drastic simplification of it. And look at the clothes of the actors depicted: they're all modern. Obviously, having made a costume drama, someone at Warner's decided that it wouldn't sell...

ABOVE RIGHT **Airport** 'The year's most awaited film.' Awaited by whom? The producer?

RIGHT **Big Deal at Dodge City** This is an especially meaningless British title for a film known in America as *A Big Hand for the Little Lady*: the action takes place entirely in Laredo, and Dodge City (many long miles away) is never even mentioned. Moreover, the suggestion of so much action and adventure is a bit cheeky in view of the fact that the film takes place almost entirely in the back room of a saloon, and although guns are brandished there is no real action at all, just humour and a little suspense.

**MEN WITHOUT BODIES!
SKULLS THAT BURN IN THE NIGHT!
INVISIBLE HANDS THAT *KILL!***

NEW HEIGHTS
OF HORROR in this
MASTERPIECE
of the MACABRE!

Night Creatures

in Eastman COLOR

Even from the coffin, no woman was safe
from the horror of the Marsh Phantoms!

Only one man knew their secret —
and torture silenced his tongue!

Starring
PETER CUSHING · YVONNE ROMAIN
PATRICK ALLEN · OLIVER REED
SCREENPLAY BY
JOHN ELDER · PETER GRAHAM SCOTT
PRODUCED BY
JOHN TEMPLE-SMITH · A Hammer-Major Production
A Universal-International Release

THE SUPREME IN HIGH ADVENTURE

...with the swindlers, suckers, sinners
and those who believe that dishonesty
is the only policy that pays!

BLAST-OFF

...formerly "THOSE FANTASTIC
FLYING FOOLS"

IN COLOR AND
PANAVISION

AMERICAN
INTERNATIONAL
STARS
BURL   TROY   GERT   HERMIONE   LIONEL DALIAH
IVES · DONAHUE · FROBE · GINGOLD · JEFFRIES · LAVI
DENNIS PRICE · STRATFORD JOHNS · GRAHAM STARK · AND TERRY-THOMAS
DIRECTED BY   PRODUCED BY   ORIGINAL STORY BY   SCREENPLAY BY
DON SHARP · HARRY ALAN TOWERS · PETER WELBECK · DAVE FREEMAN
© 1967 American International Pictures

LEFT Night Creatures *Actually a mild period adventure about a reformed pirate disguised as a village priest (based on Russell Thorndike's book Dr Syn), this pleasant British effort, known in Britain as* **Captain Clegg**, *had to disguise itself as a horror film in America. Audiences must have demanded their money back.*

BELOW LEFT Blast Off *The original title was in fact P. T. Barnum's Rocket to the Moon, intended to suggest a gentle Victorian comedy on the lines of Around The World in Eighty Days. It didn't work at the box office, so Those Fantastic Flying Fools was chosen to suggest another recent success, Those Magnificent Men in Their Flying Machines. When that didn't work either, the film was sold as an action adventure, which it certainly wasn't.*

BELOW Return of Captain America *At least they're honest this time. Any fan of Captain America who thinks he's seeing a sequel will find out if he reads the small print that its just the same serial retitled. If this kind of thing works, why bother to make new films at all?*

THE NUMBER ONE
CHOICE OF YOUNG
AND OLD —
CAPTAIN
AMERICA!

RETURN of CAPTAIN AMERICA

FORMERLY ENTITLED "CAPTAIN AMERICA"
Based on the Character appearing in CAPTAIN AMERICA COMICS

DICK PURCELL
LIONEL ATWILL
LORNA GRAY

A REPUBLIC SERIAL IN 15 CHAPTERS

BELOW **Becket** Murder is mentioned, and the scenes shown include knife fights, wild revelry, and action on horseback. Audiences found that these pleasures were only fleeting in a very long, intellectual film concerned with ecclesiastical history and personal conscience. And you would scarcely know from the ad that Becket was an archbishop!

RIGHT **The Story of Mankind** All the claims made here are pretty dubious, especially about the star cast. The cast consists mainly of character actors who would never claim that rank. The producer's theory is clearly that people will believe you if you shout loud enough.

CENTRE RIGHT **The Ten Commandments** 'Greatest entertainment of all time.' There's no answer to that… except perhaps that the Bible was not precisely intended as entertainment.

FAR RIGHT **The Last Days of Pompeii** The fiery death was not exactly from the skies, but from a volcano discharging lava. And we doubt that any cast, however mammoth, has numbered ten thousand: no budget could encompass that number of extras, and no film could need them.

RIGHT **The Egyptian** 'Only Cinemascope…'? Well, the original book encompassed it pretty well. And the 'revolutionary new anamorphic lens' was forty years old at the time: until TV threatened cinema box offices, no one had been interested in using it.

We don't say that all cinema advertising is misleading. But some of it is.
We suggest that you should use your common sense when reading it.

Tom Mix

The First Cowboy ★ Stars ★ ★ ★

Back in 1903, when the cinema was still very young, audiences were excited by a new film that was really quite different from anything they had so far seen. It was called *The Great Train Robbery* and it had been made by Edwin S. Porter for the Edison Company, in New York. There were a number of things that made *The Great Train Robbery* stand out from the other films of that time. For a start it was longer running: it ran for just on ten minutes, which was quite a long time for a film in those days. And, even more important, it told a story.

That may not seem very unusual to us now, but you have to remember that in the early days of the cinema most films were nothing more than simple records of everyday events and scenes. *The Great Train Robbery* told the story of a train hold-up by a gang of bandits, their escape with the loot, and finally their tracking down and defeat in a gun battle by the forces of law and order. Although most of the film was shot in New Jersey just outside New York, it was supposed to take place in the far west and its story of crime, pursuit and capture set the pattern for the thousands of western films that have followed it.

The one thing *The Great Train Robbery* lacked was a hero: a single identifiable cowboy character who could defeat the villains. Yet, in a way, this important film even helped to provide this missing ingredient. One of the actors who played a couple of very small parts in *The Great Train Robbery* was called G. M. Anderson. It was in fact his first film and seeing its tremendous success he decided that movies were the business for him. Over the next few years he worked on several films, sometimes as actor, sometimes as director. Eventually he formed his own film company in Chicago called the Essanay Company. In 1908 he moved to California and decided to make westerns, but with a difference. Most of the western films that had followed *The Great Train Robbery* had been failures, and Anderson came to the conclusion that this was because there had been no central character in them which the audience could like and support. He decided to create a cowboy hero. Unable to find a suitable actor he decided, in desperation, to appear in the first film himself, which was called *Broncho Billy and the Baby*. It was a tremendous success and convinced Anderson not only that he should go on making westerns, but that he should keep the character of Broncho Billy. Over the next few years he made nearly five hundred short Broncho Billy films and in the process became the cinema's very first cowboy star. By 1915 other western stars were replacing Broncho Billy Anderson and in the early 1920s he retired from films completely,

A scene from one of the world's first story films, The Great Train Robbery, made in 1903.

William S. Hart in action in a saloon setting which accurately reproduces the real thing.

'Broncho Billy' Anderson

but he was to enjoy a long retirement living to the ripe old age of ninety.

In 1911, when Broncho Billy Anderson was at the peak of his career, a new cowboy hero made his first screen appearance. His name was Tom Mix. Where the Broncho Billy character had been rather stern and reasonably realistic in its portrayal of the westerner, Tom Mix's cowboy was much slicker and more glamorized. The Tom Mix costume was fancier and far more elaborate than any genuine working cowboy would have worn and included beautifully embroidered shirts and trousers decorated with gold braid. Unlike Anderson, however, Tom Mix had been a real cowboy at one time. His career before starting in movies had in fact been as adventurous as many of the films he was to make. While still in his teens he had joined the US army and seen action in the Spanish-American War. Later he fought at Peking in China during the Boxer rebellion. When he left the army he became a horse-breaker and spent some time with the British army in South Africa during the Boer War. Back in America he moved to the west where he became, in succession, a cowboy, rodeo performer, Texas ranger, sheriff and eventually deputy US marshal for the eastern division of Oklahoma. He first drifted into films as general advisor and animal-handler on a western and was soon both directing and starring in his own short films of which he made nearly a hundred in the years between 1911 and 1917. In that year he switched to feature films and was to carry on right into the 1930s. He made his screen farewell in 1935 with a western serial called *The Miracle Rider* and then went on tour with his own wild animal circus. In October 1940 he was killed in a car accident near Florence, Arizona, and a statue of a riderless pony now stands there to mark where he died.

The third great cowboy star of the silent screen was William Surrey Hart, and, although he arrived on the scene after Broncho Billy Anderson and his career was much shorter than that of Tom Mix, he made the greatest contribution to the development of the western films of the three. He was born in 1870 in New York, but as a small boy he went with his family to live in Dakota, where they settled near an Indian reservation. Here he played with Sioux children and learned their language. When he was older he worked as a cowboy in Kansas but eventually the family had to return to New York. Here Hart became an actor and first played a western role in stage productions of *The Squaw Man* and *The Virginian*. It was whilst on tour in 1914 with the play *The Trail of the Lonesome Pine* that he reached California and met up again with an old actor friend, Thomas Ince. Ince by now was an important film-maker with his own studios and Hart was soon busy making westerns for him. Right from the start Hart, who had an intense love of the west, was determined that his films should be absolutely realistic and portray the west and the western way of life as accurately as possible. He directed all his own films and within a year they had become enormously popular with cinema audiences. Over the next few years he became Hollywood's undisputed leading cowboy star with very many films to his credit. His last one, *Tumbleweeds*, came in 1925, after which he retired from films. His close friends included such real life western lawmen as Wyatt Earp and Bat Masterson. He died in 1946 and his ranch is now a museum of western history containing the valuable collection of costumes, guns and saddles which he collected during his lifetime.

PRESERVING FILMS FOR POSTERITY
The Work of a Film Archive

People have been making films for nearly eighty years, so you would expect there to be an awful lot of film in the world by now. And you would be right: there *is* an awful lot of film in the world, but not quite so much as there should be. You see, in the cinema's early days most people, including the early film-makers themselves, didn't regard the films they had made as particularly important, and certainly never imagined that they could be of any historical significance. So they made no effort to keep them once their commercial usefulness was over, and that is a sad loss for historians.

Movie film itself is comparatively fragile—it is very easily scratched or torn. Even worse, for the first fifty years of the life of the cinema, film was made of a highly inflammable material called cellulose nitrate. Not only does nitrate film, as it was known, burn very readily, but

Traffic jams are nothing new. This scene of a London street crammed with horse transport of every kind was filmed in 1896, and comes from one of the very first films ever made in London.

unless it is carefully stored and looked after, it eventually starts to decompose and turn into a messy jelly-like substance. It's not surprising, therefore, that much of the film shot during the years 1895 to 1910 has been lost to us forever, and even many films made in later years have met a similar fate.

Today, of course, we realize the value of film and how important it is that as much as possible should be preserved for future generations to see and study. In many countries now there are archives, like our own National Film Archive, where films are carefully stored at the correct temperature, in air-conditioned vaults. At

regular intervals laboratory staff inspect the film, and, if any deterioration has taken place, a new copy of the film is made. Slowly, as money becomes available, all the existing old nitrate films are being copied onto modern safety film. This has a much longer life, and, as you might expect from its name, doesn't burn anything like as readily as the old film. But, as we said at the beginning, an awful lot of film does exist in the world. Where is it all ? Well, we've already mentioned the various film archives. These are usually run by the government or government-aided bodies. The National Film Archive, for instance, is operated by the British Film Institute.

The archives, of course, have neither the space nor the money to preserve every film, so they select films which they consider to be particularly important. These can be new films or perhaps rare copies of old films which are suddenly discovered or given to them.

ABOVE *One of the earliest films of a famous sportsman. The legendary English cricketer W. G. Grace filmed practising at the nets in 1896.*

BELOW *The newsfilm archives contain valuable film records of many famous personalities of the twentieth century. King Edward VII and Queen Alexandra leaving Dartmouth Naval College in 1905.*

The major film companies themselves also keep libraries of their old films, more so these days than in past years because of the possibility of selling them to television. But of course film companies can go out of business, so it is vital that the various national archives exist.

There is another and particularly interesting type of film library or archive, of which there

ABOVE RIGHT *The year is 1905 and Theodore Roosevelt, the president of the United States, prepares to make a flight in the Wright brothers' new-fangled flying machine. Roosevelt was the first head of state in the world to fly and the early newsreel cameras were there to record the historic event.*

RIGHT *The Empire Theatre in Leicester Square, London, around the turn of the century. Notice the sign on the front of the theatre advertising the 'Lumière Cinematographie'. Many of the first public film shows were staged as part of a music hall bill.*

BELOW *In 1911 King George V and Queen Mary went to India to be crowned emperor and empress. At Delhi an enormous Durbar was staged with thousands of troops and the colourful Indian princes taking part.*

News films of the Great War did much to increase the importance of the cinema. British troops go into action in the battle of the Somme in 1916.

are quite a number around the world. These are the libraries of the various newsreel companies. Nowadays, it is very rare for a newsreel to be included in a cinema programme, but for more than half a century they provided people with their only means of actually seeing important, and sometimes not so important, events, until, of course, the television news programmes took their place. From the cinema's earliest days movie cameras had been used to make records of events like horse races and great state occasions. The Diamond Jubilee procession of Queen Victoria in 1898 was filmed by several cameramen, as was her funeral in 1902. But it was not until 1910 that the first regular weekly

Audiences were anxious to see their movie idols as often as possible. Here two of Hollywood's greatest silent stars, Douglas Fairbanks and Mary Pickford, are filmed for Pathé News on a visit to London in 1920.

newsreel appeared. It was made by the French Pathé Company and they set up an office in London to produce an English edition also. They called it Pathé's Animated Gazette. The Gaumont Company, also French, quickly followed with their reel called the Gaumont Graphic. It was obviously thought to be a good thing to have a title that sounded like a newspaper. In the years that followed various other newsreels appeared. Some, like Topical Budget, lasted a comparatively short time, while others were to continue right into the television age. They included Paramount News (run by Paramount Pictures) and the Fox Film Company newsreel, Movietone News. This was the first

Here crowds celebrate as the first news of an armistice reaches London in November 1918.

newsreel to use sound, and its British offshoot British Movietone News is still in existence, the only cinema newsreel left in this country. Similar reels existed in other countries. America, France of course, and Germany all had particularly good ones.

Most newsreels appeared in two separate editions every week, each edition usually running for about eight to ten minutes. Multiply this by fifty years or so and you'll begin to get some idea of how much newsfilm there is in the world. When you realize that this film covers virtually the entire history of our century you'll appreciate its enormous importance. Fortunately, a great deal of it has been reasonably well preserved and catalogued. This is especially important because, with such large quantities of film, unless careful records are kept it would be quite impossible to find any particular item.

Let's look in a little more detail at one particular library, that of Pathé News, the one which, to date, has covered the longest period of time. We have already seen how it started in 1910 as Pathé's Animated Gazette. It went through various changes of name until just after the Second World War it eventually became simply Pathé News. It appeared for the last time in February 1970. For most of these sixty years, in addition to the two weekly editions of the news, Pathé also produced a weekly film

In 1929 an attempt to achieve the long sought after goal of man-powered flight. As you might have guessed, it did not succeed.

Not a scene from a Warner Brothers gangster film, but an actual newsreel of 1930 showing machine-gun-carrying cops, in hot pursuit of hoodlums.

magazine called Pathé Pictorial. This also ran for about ten minutes and consisted usually of lighter general interest and travel items. It is these several thousand newsreels and pictorials which make up the present Pathé Film Library, now incidentally a part of the giant EMI company. Film in this quantity presents quite a storage problem, the more so when you realize that for each newsreel there is usually a reel of picture negative, a reel of soundtrack negative and a positive print. In addition to the reels themselves there are also hundreds of thousands of feet of 'unused film'. That is film shot by the cameramen, which for various reasons was

never actually included in an issued newsreel, but which may nevertheless contain important or interesting events.

The Pathé Film Library is situated in the heart of London's filmland, in Wardour Street, Soho, although not all of the vast amount of film they hold can be kept there. Much of this, including all the negatives, is stored in specially constructed vaults at the EMI Film Studios in Elstree, about ten miles from the centre of London. In Wardour Street are kept those films which are most frequently used, together with the viewing machines and the index system which provides the vital catalogue of all the films in the library.

The crash of the giant German airship Hindenburg *in the United States in 1937. A fairly rare example of a tragic disaster filmed as it actually happened. For obvious reasons the newsreel coverage of events such as this generally consists only of scenes of the aftermath.*

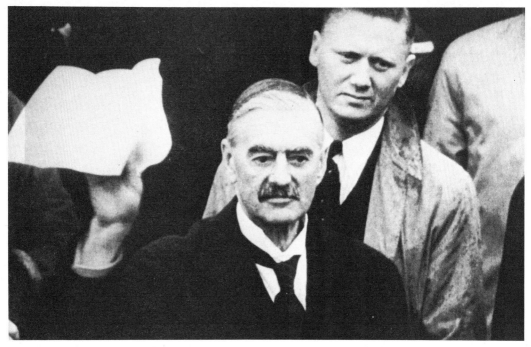

ABOVE *Prime Minister Neville Chamberlain returns from Munich in 1938 proudly displaying the famous bit of paper, an agreement signed with Hitler which brought, so the people hoped, 'peace in our time'.*

BELOW *The Second World War, and newsreel cameras are busy at the Dunkirk beaches in 1940. A scene from the only film of this historic event, shot by Charles Martin of Pathé News.*

ABOVE *The destruction of the United States fleet at Pearl Harbour in the Pacific by Japanese planes in 1942.*

BELOW *Britain's great war-time prime minister, Winston Churchill, with Joseph Stalin, the Russian leader in 1942.*

The index works like this. Every newsreel has a reference number made up from its year and its edition number. For example, the first reel produced in 1938 would be simply 1/38. The reel issued at the end of January would be 8/38 (because two reels were issued every week) and so on right through the year. The tins containing the reels are, of course, marked accordingly, and stored on racks in date order. It's a fairly simple matter, therefore, to find the newsreel relating to any particular period. If you want to see what was happening in, say, February 1947, you pull out all the tins marked 9/47 to 16/47. But mostly the film librarian's life is not as easy as this. More often than not he is called on to find all the bits of film relating to some famous person, or perhaps he is asked to produce film shots of a foreign city or maybe of some manufacturing process. This is where the index system becomes so important. Over the years the film librarians have listed on cards the complete contents of each of the newsreels, under various subject headings. For instance one section of the index is labelled 'Personalities'. On these cards, in alphabetical order, are the names of all the important people who appear in the reels, together with a brief description of

what they are doing, and followed by the reference number of the reel. Another section is labelled 'Locations', which simply means places. This one is divided again into countries, and then yet again into names of important towns. If you wanted to find some film showing scenes of New York, you would go to the index drawer marked Locations and look through the cards for the section marked USA, in which you would find a smaller group marked New York. From these cards you could read a description of all the film in the library which shows views of New York. The next stage, of course, would be to get out the actual reels containing the various shots and look at them on one of the film-viewing machines.

The television companies in particular make a great deal of use of the newsreel libraries. You have probably seen many programmes such as 'All Our Yesterdays' which consist entirely of old newsfilm. We should explain, of course, that only copies of the films are used in programmes such as these. The original reels are kept intact, to be preserved we hope forever. No doubt in the year 2000 TV programmes and films will be produced from today's newsfilm, held in the rapidly growing libraries of the television news organizations.

Part of the extensive card index at the Pathé Film Library on which are recorded details of the millions of feet of film preserved in their vaults.

An example of one of the record cards.

....AVIATION........................**Main**......RECORD FLIGHTS & STUNTS............**Sub.**	
DETAILS	LIBRARY NO. AND DATE
JERRIE MOCK FLIES SOLO AROUND THE WORLD (Oakland U.S.A.) VS. Mrs. Jerrie Mock poses by her single engine plane, "Spirit of Columbia". MS.It starts up and begins to taxi. LS. Pan of the aircraft taking off from a Texas airport. VS. At night a crowd acclaim Jerrie Mock on her arrival back home at Ohio Airport. (Comb.F.G.)	3890.C. 28.4.64
JOAN MERRIAM FLIES SOLO AROUND WORLD (California) LS.Pan as small plane lands on runway.VS.The small plane 'City of Long Beach' comes to a standstill and Miss Joan Merriam steps out and is greeted after her solo round the world flight.VS.Miss Merriam meeting the press in the airport building. (Comb.F.G.)	3891.D. 14.5.64
STUNT FLYING IN GERMANY - RENDSBURG VS.Stunt planes performing loop the loop and barrel rolls, etc. and the stunt flying winner is Gerhard Pawolka. (Comb.F.G.)	3925.E. 21.8.64
TEST FLIGHTS FOR NEW T.S.R.2 (Boscombe Down) VS. The two pilots take up their positions in the two cockpits and prepare for test flight. LS.Pan as TSR-2 gathers speed and then lets her parachute go to slow her down. LS.Pan TSR 2 gathers speed and takes off and heads into the sky. LS.Ground to air of TSR-2 in flight. LS.Of TSR-2 coming in to land and landing, it stops by letting her drag-chute go. (Dupe.)	3940.B. 16.9.64
RED ARROWS WARM UP - LITTLE RISSINGTON (SEE CARD - AVIATION - AIR DISPLAYS) (Orig.Neg.)	65/38 9.5.65

HOW FILMS
FOUND THEIR VOICE

Although talking pictures, as we know them today, did not generally reach the cinemas until the end of the 1920s, experiments to link sound with moving pictures had been going on since the cinema's earliest days.

Round about the year 1888 William Friese-Greene (see p. 19) had sent details of his film projector to Thomas Edison in America with the suggestion that it might be possible to link the projector with Edison's cylinder gramophone (or phonograph) to produce talking pictures. Nothing came of that particular idea but a few years later, in 1893, at the Chicago World Exposition, Edison demonstrated his kinetophonograph, which was a combination of his peepshow machine, the kinetoscope, and his phonograph; while in France in 1896 the Pathé Company used the then newly invented gramophone discs to add a sound accompaniment to some of their films. In the years that followed many similar systems appeared with such names as the 'Vivaphone' and the 'Cinephone'. Some of them had limited demonstrations in cinemas and theatres but nobody really took them very seriously or saw them as any sort of threat to silent pictures. In 1910 the Edison Company produced a whole series of short musical films featuring opera and vaudeville performers, with the sound recorded on phonograph cylinders.

ABOVE *The film that changed the history of the movies*—The Jazz Singer. *When during the making of the film Jolson burst out with 'you ain't heard nothing yet' Sam Warner realized the tremendous impact the spoken word would have on audiences. He immediately had a short speech written for Jolson to say to his mother (played by Eugenie Besserer) during the musical number 'Blue Skies'. The photograph shows a moment from that scene.*

However these films, in common with all the other early talkies, had two main problems. The first was making the sound loud enough to be heard in large halls or theatres. (It was not until many years later that the invention of the thermionic valve made possible the building of sound amplifiers.) The second was the synchronizing of sound and picture, which simply means making the sound match perfectly with the picture. When in a film someone closes a door, you expect to hear the sound of the door closing at exactly the same time as you see it happen. When an actor speaks, his lip movements must exactly match the words he is saying. To synchronize gramophone records or phonograph cylinders to film was quite difficult, and various mechanical systems were devised in an attempt to overcome the problem. One of the more incredible-sounding systems actually used a shaft which ran the whole length of the hall linking the projector at the back of the hall to the gramophone placed by the screen. None of them were ever completely successful. The

Thomas Edison's equipment for making early talkies. The large box-like piece of equipment on the right is the camera or kinetograph, as Edison called it. On the left is the phonograph linked to the camera by electrical wires so that some sort of synchronization could be obtained between the two. There were no microphones as we know them today, so the performers would have to speak very loudly for their voices to be picked up by the large horn of the phonograph.

simplest and most trouble-free system would obviously be to record the sound photographically alongside the picture on the one strip of film, then sound and picture would always remain perfectly in step. This is what eventually happened (a thin shaft of light acts like the needle on a record player) and is the method used to this day.

Towards the end of the nineteenth century several scientists including Alexander Graham Bell, the inventor of the telephone, had experimented with ways of changing sound waves into light waves, but it was in England in 1907 that Eugene Lauste devised a method of photographing these light waves onto movie film. His invention is described in the records of the British patent office as 'a means for recording and reproducing simultaneously the movements or motions of persons or objects and the sounds produced by them...so that the impressions of the movements would be recorded simultaneously with the impression of the sound waves and will be reproduced simultaneously and in exact synchronism with them'. In other words, Eugene Lauste had invented talking pictures as we know them today. Lauste, unfortunately, was dogged by the old problem of being unable to make his film sound recordings loud enough for public shows, and, like Friese-Greene before him, he ran out of money. Another very important name is that of the American scientist Lee De Forest. He made a double contribution really, because not only

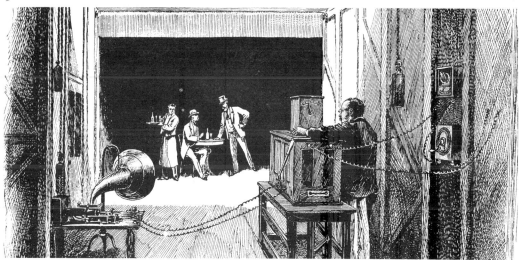

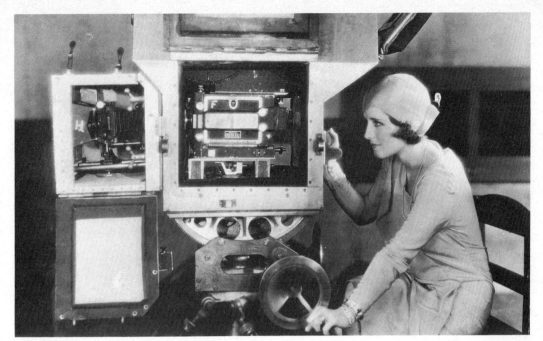

Norma Shearer, famous Hollywood star of the thirties, with one of the first 'sound proof' cameras. In the early days of sound, cameras were fixed in glass booths to prevent the noise they made reaching the microphones. But later, cameras were placed in sound proof boxes or 'blimps' enabling them to become mobile again, as in the days of silent films.

did he devise a method of recording sound on film, but he also solved the loudness problem: he invented the thermionic valve, thus making possible the building of sound amplifiers. He called his system Phonofilm and in 1923 he successfully demonstrated it in public with a number of short films featuring orchestras and singers. The film industry, however, showed little interest in the novelty. As long as audiences were satisfied with silent films there did not seem any point in going to the expense of re-equipping cinemas and studios for sound. Then, in the mid-twenties, the movies were faced with competition from a new form of entertainment – radio. People began to stay at home, enraptured by the sound of voices coming over the loudspeakers of their radio sets. The film industry needed something new to bring back the audiences and, as it appeared to be voices they wanted, the obvious answer was talking pictures. The company that finally took

the plunge was Warner Brothers. Unlike the other major American film studios, Warners did not have their own chain of cinemas, so to get their films shown they had to offer something different. On 6 August 1926, to an enthusiastic audience, they premièred their first full-length sound film, *Don Juan*. Starring John Barrymore, it had a synchronized sound-track consisting only of music and sound effects. Film-goers had to wait another year before they heard speech in a feature film. That film was *The Jazz Singer*, which had its première in New York on 6 October 1927, and the speech audiences heard was really the result of an accident. Warner Brothers had only intended the film to have songs by its star Al Jolson, but during the recording of one of the songs Jolson burst out 'Wait a minute, folks, you ain't heard nothing yet, listen to this'. Sam Warner, who was supervising the recording, decided to leave these sentences in the picture and also arranged for some additional dialogue to be recorded by Jolson for another scene. When the film was shown in public these few sentences, even more than the songs, had a tremendous impact on film-goers. The movies had found their voice.

Surprisingly, Warners did not use De Forest's Phonofilm system for their first sound

The dubbing theatre at the EMI-Elstree Studios. The technicians seated at the control panel can watch the film on the screen and mix the various soundtracks together in exact synchronization with the picture.

films. Instead they used the much more cumbersome method of synchronizing gramophone records to film, which had been developed by the Bell Telephone Laboratories. It was called Vitaphone. Early in 1928 another Hollywood studio, Fox, introduced their own sound system called Movietone. This was very similar to Lee De Forest's process with the sound track recorded photographically on the edge of the film, the method eventually used by all the studios including Warners.

The success of *The Jazz Singer* sparked off a rush by the whole film industry to turn over to the production of talking pictures. Half-completed silent films were abandoned or hastily re-shot as talkies. Some famous names of the silent screen, who turned out to have poor speaking voices, disappeared from the movies forever, and experienced stage actors and singers were soon in great demand by the

Hollywood studios. In England the race to bring out the first British talkie was won by Alfred Hitchcock. He was filming a thriller, silent of course, at Elstree Film Studios, when the sound revolution happened. Film sound equipment was in short supply but Hitchcock obtained some and re-shot with sound the sequences already completed. The title of the film was *Blackmail* and it was completed in 1929.

In the fifty years that have passed since Lee De Forest's Phonofilm shorts, the science and art of sound recording has made enormous progress. New techniques, in particular the introduction of magnetic sound recordings, have made possible the present very high standard of most film soundtracks.

The modern soundtrack is made up of several different layers of sounds, all generally recorded quite separately. First of all there is the dialogue. This means the words spoken by the actors, and it is normally recorded at the same time as the film is shot, on magnetic tape fed into a machine basically the same as a domestic tape-recorder. Camera and recorder are linked together so that sound and picture

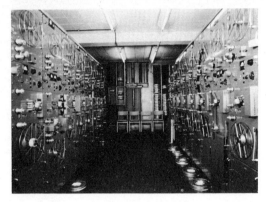

The banks of playback and recording machines situated in a room adjoining the dubbing theatre. They can all be started, stopped and run forward or backwards by remote control from the panel in the dubbing theatre. The machines are interlocked with each other and the film projector so that perfect synchronization of all the separate soundtracks and the picture film is maintained at all times.

will be in perfect synchronization; and to make sure they start that way a 'clapperboard' is used. This is a small wooden board on which is written, usually in chalk, the number of the scene being filmed. A piece of wood is hinged to the top of the board in such a way that it can be lifted and then closed to produce a sharp bang. At the beginning of each shot, or scene, that goes to make up a film, an assistant holds up the clapperboard in front of the camera. As soon as the camera and sound-recorder are running he closes the top hinged part and makes a bang. He then quickly steps out of the way, removing the board, and with camera and recorder still running the scene is filmed. When, later on, the two pieces of film, one containing the

A strip of combined or 'married' film with the soundtrack printed alongside the picture. The wavy white line is the track and it is through this that a narrow beam of light is projected onto a photo-electric cell. The cell converts the varying light impulses back into sound waves.

picture and the other the soundtrack, are given to the film editor, he is able to see on the film and hear on the soundtrack the precise point at which the hinged part of the clapperboard hits the board itself. He can match the two exactly together and, of course, the rest of the scene will then match as well. The bits of film and track containing the clapperboard are then cut off and thrown away.

As well as dialogue, film soundtracks invariably contain various sound effects. These can be anything from pistol shots to wind howling through the trees. Sounds such as pistol shots or doors slamming are called 'spot effects' because they have to be synchronized exactly to the picture. Other noises, like wind or rain, or perhaps traffic heard from inside a house, don't have to match the picture quite so closely. All

Sound tracks are generally recorded during or after filming. Cartoons are the exception, with the sound track being recorded first and the drawings done to fit the sound. In this picture Peggy Lee is recording the siamese cats' song for the Disney feature cartoon **The Lady and the Tramp.**

these various sounds, however, are recorded quite separately and reach the editor on yet another strip of film.

Finally, there is the background music. This is recorded when all the film has been shot and the editor has cut and assembled the picture more or less into its final form and length. All these various soundtracks are now assembled together by the dubbing editor and it's his job to make sure that each piece of sound matches its correct picture. At the end of this process, for every reel of picture there will be at least three separate reels of soundtrack. Picture and tracks are now sent to the dubbing theatre. Here the separate tracks are mixed and blended together and re-recorded onto a single track. At this stage, picture and sound are still on separate reels, and the soundtrack is still on magnetic film. Now it has to be re-recorded yet again, this time to produce a photographic or optical soundtrack, as it is usually called. Finally this optical soundtrack and the picture film are printed together to produce picture and sound side by side on the one strip of film. At last it is ready to be shown in your local cinema.

Happy Families
Ma, Pa and the Kids on Film

Throughout our lives, the family is the most important society we live in. We learn more about the problems of growing up from our mother, father, brothers and sisters than from anyone else, and, even if we disagree with them sometimes, a special relationship builds up. This can never be replaced, except by our relationship with the family which we ourselves may start. A happy family is a great thing to be part of.

These days, families tend to split up much earlier than they used to: children become independent at an earlier age, and so much information is available from school, from books and from television that they do not need or demand so much family guidance; indeed they often resent it. The result is sometimes unhappiness, but that seems to be the way of the world.

It was not always so. During the hundred years up to the Second World War, people had more children, and the family was a massive complex unit of which everyone was proud to be a member. For entertainment in Victorian

ABOVE **A Family Affair** *This 1936 second feature was the first of the enormously successful Hardy family films, representing life in middle-class America. Furnishings accurately depicted a comfortable, even well-to-do home of the times, though Judge Hardy (Lionel Barrymore) might have been expected to choose a more comfortable chair with less jazzy upholstery. Mickey Rooney (standing by the fireplace) and Sara Haden (seated with her back to the* window) *stayed on to become mainstays of the series. But Spring Byington (seated facing Barrymore) preferred to play mother to another film family, the Joneses, shown on page 16. The Jones films were on a lower level of comedy, but they pleased a lot of people. Jed Prouty, an amiable old character actor, was given his biggest chance as a father, and played the role to the hilt. Both series continued well into World War II, reminding servicemen of home.*

times there would be family musical evenings, with each performing on his own instrument; in Edwardian times father used to take his troop to the theatre or music hall; in the thirties he would organize a family party to the cinema (it was much cheaper then). Right up to the time of their marriage, children were pleased to accompany their parents unless they had a 'date'. Naturally the film-makers knew this, and ensured that their films as well as their theatres had family appeal. One obvious way was to make films about ideal families, and a number of series of this kind, which today would seem

ABOVE **Andy Hardy's Double Life** *Here are the Hardys in 1942, when they were established as America's number one box office attraction and were doing pretty well in the rest of the world. From the lettering on the mailbox this seems to be a posed still for overseas fans; the picket fence would be especially nostalgic to forces serving abroad. The family regulars pictured are Fay Holden (actually British by birth), Mickey Rooney, Lewis Stone, Cecilia Parker and Sara Haden.*

BELOW **Four Men and a Prayer** *At least a couple of these well-scrubbed faces must be familiar. In 1938 they were all starters in a Hollywood film about four brothers getting together to avenge the death of their father. From left to right: Richard Greene, who later became familiar as television's Robin Hood; George Sanders, suave villain of innumerable films; David Niven, perennial superstar; and William Henry, a former American child actor whose adult career never really took him to the top.*

impossibly sentimental, tame or stuffy, were then tremendously popular.

Paramount among them were the Hardys. They started off in 1936 in a single film called *A Family Affair*, designed as a supporting feature. The story was all about minor incidents in the family of a small-town mid-western judge, played by Lionel Barrymore. It caused little stir, and when MGM thought a second film about the Hardys might make a useful second feature for the following year, Lionel Barrymore hastily bowed out and was replaced by Lewis Stone—who remained for more episodes. The rest of the family was signed up under long-term contract: Fay Holden (originally British) as Mrs Hardy, Cecilia Parker as her daughter, Sara Haden as her spinster sister, and above all Mickey Rooney as her teenage son Andy, who was always getting into trouble. Well, the series took off like a rocket, largely because of ebullient young Mr Rooney and his man-to-man talks with his wise if elderly dad. The enormous popularity of the series all over the world was like the last burst of old-fashioned family sentiment before war broke out. MGM were delighted. The series was cheap and easy to make, it was good for prestige (it depicted in a rosy glow the kind of ordinary American family towards whom President Roosevelt was addressing his New Deal), and it was a good testing ground for new talent, especially starlets who could be used as girl-friends for Andy. (Ava Gardner and Judy Garland were among those who passed this way.) All through the war the Hardys rode high, producing an image of America which all the world accepted; then suddenly Mickey Rooney, who had been number one at the box office, lost his appeal, having become too old to convince as a teenager. By the time he came back from war, the easy do-gooder philosophy of the Hardys had given way to a tougher look at the world. The films were never revived. Lewis Stone died in 1953, and when in 1958 an attempt was made to restart the series without him (*Andy Hardy Comes Home*) it was all as dead as mutton.

Meanwhile the other Hollywood studios had not been slow to start families of their own. At Fox, the Joneses were set in precisely the same

The Young in Heart *Families could be lovable even if they were not quite admirable. The Carletons in this 1939 film are in fact a family of confidence tricksters out to swindle the old lady (Minnie Dupree) out of as many of her millions as they can. But this was a comedy, and they reform in the end. Father is Roland Young, England's gift to Hollywood in the thirties and forties: he always seemed to have a smile on his lips, and his murmuring voice was enjoyed by millions. Equally delightful was Billie Burke (left), world-famous Broadway beauty of an earlier age who found a niche in Hollywood as a delightful ditherer. Janet Gaynor (right) was a big star of the twenties and thirties, but after* The Young in Heart *she retired, making only a single comeback in the fifties in a mother role.*

milieu as the Hardys; Dad (Jed Prouty) was mayor instead of judge, and he had an elderly mother (Florence Roberts) instead of a spinster sister, but otherwise it was much the same except that Prouty and Spring Byington, who played Mrs Jones, were comedians by nature and played closer to farce than to comedy. For this reason, perhaps, the Joneses never rose above second feature level, but they were fun all the same. Actually the Jones family had started in 1931, with a somewhat different cast; but in 1936 they staged a determined comeback and between then and 1940 appeared in fifteen films.

Even closer to farce, really on the level of the newspaper comic strip in which they originated, were the Bumsteads of *Blondie*, begun in 1938. Here we moved into suburbia: Dagwood, played by Arthur Lake with a strange centre

Since You Went Away *A group of forties superstars appeared in this very long and sentimental tribute to the American family at war while Dad was away fighting the Nazis. One criticism was that this particular family didn't seem to suffer much. Joseph Cotten played the understanding friend, the daughters are Jennifer Jones and Shirley Temple (compare her at the age of sixteen with the picture of her at twelve on page 118), and Claudette Colbert was mother.*

---

parting and a general air of stupefaction, was the young family man who kept falling over things and getting in trouble with his boss, Mr Dithers; but of course he came out on top in the end, more by luck than by judgment. The other stars were Larry Simms, as Baby Dumpling; Daisy the dog; and, as Dagwood's pretty wife Blondie, Penny Singleton, who despite being top-billed had really least to do. The most cherished image from this Columbia series, which went on until 1948 and produced twenty films, was the much-repeated scene of Dagwood gulping down his breakfast and dashing from the house to catch his train. Inevitably we next heard a thud and an anguished cry as he bumped into the long-suffering postman, who

would then be seen lying on the path as a shower of letters descended about him.

Other shorter-lived family series included *Four Daughters*, *Four Wives* and *Four Mothers*, with the real-life Lane sisters; and *Dear Ruth*, *Dear Wife* and *Dear Brat*, with Edward Arnold leading the Wilkinses.

British studios made several efforts to start a domestic series, but none caught on, oddly enough, until after the war, when Americans were looking for other subjects. In 1948 British audiences flocked to see Rank's *Here Come the Huggetts*. The level here was somewhere between the Joneses and the Hardys; plenty of fun, but an air of gritty realism behind it. For the Huggetts, unlike their American counterparts, were staunchly working-class, indelibly personified by Jack Warner and Kathleen Harrison, who could never entirely shake off the characterizations although only four films were made. The teenage children were played by Susan Shaw and Jimmy Hanley, and, as with the Hardys, many young British actors and actresses were tried out in supporting parts.

Apart from series, a great many single films have been made about families. During the war it was good propaganda for families to stand together and defend their traditions. *Forever and a Day* traced the lineage of a British family back to the eighteenth century. Noel Coward's *This Happy Breed* showed the development of a British family between the two wars: *Cavalcade* traced one back to the Boer War. *Since You Went Away* showed the women of an American family standing firmly together waiting for Dad to come home. *The Human Comedy* and *Happy Land* were sentimental looks at American rural families where Dad *didn't* come home. *Our Town* took two small-town families and tried to make them symbolic of the human condition. *The Sullivans* were a family who lost five sons at war; *Four Sons* looked at a German family; *The Best Years of Our Lives* showed the Stephenson

family picking up the pieces of their lives after peace was declared. Later, *The Diary of Anne Frank* showed the courage and resistance of one family hiding out against the Nazis in wartime Amsterdam. *Cheaper by the Dozen*, with Clifton Webb as the efficiency expert father of a family of twelve, was the first of a number of domestic sagas on similar themes. *Dear Octopus* (the octopus was the family) dealt sympathetically with an English family of the upper middle-class; *Quiet Wedding* showed the same kind of people in a more farcical situation. *The Holly and the Ivy* described Christmas with the family of a poor rector; *It Always Rains on Sunday* had melodrama erupting in an even poorer family in London's East End. And *Grapes of Wrath* showed

Devotion *Families of classic fiction were not neglected by Hollywood, but the studios found it difficult to make an acceptable romantic film about the true story of the Brontë sisters, who lived in a bare Yorkshire parsonage with their eccentric father, wrote novels which have lasted (*Jane Eyre, Wuthering Heights*), and all died young of tuberculosis. The Brontë home is now a museum, and those who have stood in the narrow confines of its square unwelcoming rooms facing onto an old*

cemetery will laugh at this picture from the 1943 film, showing expensive furniture and trappings in a huge L-shaped room with a grand piano, wide windows and a cleverly lit inglenook fireplace. Such was the way of Hollywood then. Nowadays absolute realism would be sought, even demanded. Depicted are Montagu Love as Mr Brontë, Ida Lupino as Emily, Olivia de Havilland as Charlotte, Ethel Griffies as Aunt Branwell, Nancy Coleman as Anne. All performed well under the circumstances.

The Garnett Saga *The most typical film family of the seventies has proved to be the Garnetts of ' Till Death Do Us Part', and that just goes to show how times have changed. Instead of giving us families to look up to and respect, the entertainment media now present a scruffy working-class home in which idleness is the keynote, apart from Dad who is a loud-mouthed bigot. We all laugh at the Garnetts, but we don't sympathize with them. Not at first, anyway. But it is worth asking yourself whether any of their deplorable attitudes have rubbed off on you.*

an Oklahoma farming family sticking together under the most appalling conditions of hardship and rough treatment.

Oddly enough films have produced a number of slightly crazy or at least zany families, as though the taint of madness were always hereditary. Evil or sinister families appeared in *The Old Dark House*, *The Anniversary*, *An Inspector Calls*, *House of Strangers*, and *The Little Foxes*: the Carletons in *The Young at Heart* were ingratiating confidence tricksters. Harmlessly odd families were found in *Merrily We Go to Hell*, *Three Cornered Moon*, *The Royal Family of Broadway*, *You Can't Take it With You*, *My Man Godfrey*, *The Philadelphia Story* and *Tobacco Road*. Then there were vaudeville acts, always conceived by Hollywood as having great family loyalty: *The Merry Monahans*, *There's No Business Like Show Business*, *The Seven Little Foys*, *Yankee Doodle*

Dandy. (In the last named, George M. Cohan always finished his act as follows: 'My father thanks you, my mother thanks you, my sister thanks you, and I thank you.')

Moving closer to classical territory, many celebrated authors have written of families and had their works adapted for the screen. *Giant* depicted a Texas ranching family. *The Swiss Family Robinson* showed a family working together to combat the dangers of being ship-wrecked on a desert island. *Wuthering Heights* is basically about the interweaving of two families. *The Forsyte Saga* shows the power, rooted in trade, of a new rich family of Edwardian times. *Pride and Prejudice* takes a light-hearted look at a middle-class family living in the home counties during Napoleonic times. *Whiteoaks* was the name of a Canadian family viewed down three generations. And *Little Women* is perhaps the snuggest family of all, riddling with senti-mentality its picture of American life in the mid-nineteenth century; but it has lasted over a hundred years in public favour, so perhaps, de-spite the sophistication of the times we live in, that is the image of the family we really like to keep, with all its members coming together at Christmas and in times of crisis, and thinking of each other before themselves. Hopefully it's a style that will one day come back in fashion, as the success of recent films such as *The Railway Children* suggests.

A GALLERY OF MONSTERS

FAIRY TALE VILLAINS FOR GROWN-UPS

Only a couple of decades ago, it would have been thought very strange to suggest that young people might stretch their imaginations by looking at monsters. Oddly enough, American children have never been prevented from looking at horror comics, any more than we were prevented from looking at tuppenny 'bloods'. It's all a matter of degree; after all, Frankenstein stems from a literary classic, and Grimms' fairy tales contain plenty of monstrous images. Incidentally, the dictionary definition of monster is 'a being grotesquely different from the normal', and these days we're all being encouraged to have sympathy for those who are different from ourselves. Indeed, most of the movie monsters have been sympathetically portrayed, even though they had to be destroyed in the last reel.

It's our theory that if you are frightened by a movie monster, it's likely to be the fault not of what you see but of what you hear: the music track with its screeching violins is what curdles your blood and chills your spine. So you can't possibly come to harm by looking at this little gallery of monsters who have graced our screens during the last fifty years.

ABOVE **King Kong** *is perhaps the most lovable monster of them all. Created in 1932 by ingenious use of stop-frame animation, he existed as a whole only in an 18-inch-high version used for distant shots; for close-ups, giant arms and a huge head were constructed. He was the first giant animal to be devised by Hollywood since sound, and of course there have been hundreds of imitations; but none have rivalled the technical perfection of Kong, rampaging cutely about his jungle home or terrorizing New York when brought there (no one explained how this could be done in secret) as a music hall attraction. Sequels never caught the thrill or the professionalism of the original.*

The Creature From the Black Lagoon A tedious monster this, despite his initially splendid appearance. Also known as the 'gill man', he enlivened an otherwise boring 1954 film about an expedition up the Amazon to track down a legendary (and scientifically impossible) creature who was supposedly half man, half fish, but looked just like fellow in a plastic diving suit. The creature suffer from facial immobility, lack of speech, and t absence of traditional lore behind him; he was pr sented as little more than a wild beast. Still, spawned two sequels.

RIGHT AND FAR RIGHT **The Wolf Man** Five years after Werewolf of London, *Universal* did a complete rewrite featuring their new 'master character actor' Lon Chaney Jnr, and came up with some additions to the legend. Now it was gypsies who harboured the dread secret of were-wolfery, and when one of them bit the heir to the local manor he grew real fur and fangs. (Mr Chaney was more willing than Mr Hull had been to submit to four hours of painful and boring make-up each day.) In this film it appeared that the wolf man could be killed only by repeated blows from a wolf-head-topped silver cane; but in the inevitable sequels this was changed to a silver bullet. Even this, fired as per the legend by one who loved him, did not keep Mr Chaney down, and in 1945, in House of Dracula, he was 'cured' by surgery; but three years later he popped up again to bother Abbott and Costello. In one of the sequels, Franken-stein Meets the Wolf Man, Jack Pierce and the editors created a splendid sequence of lap-dissolves which seemed to show the hair actually growing on Mr Chaney's face. As late as 1962, Hammer tried a British variation, Curse of the Werewolf, with Oliver Reed, but it substituted nastiness for style.

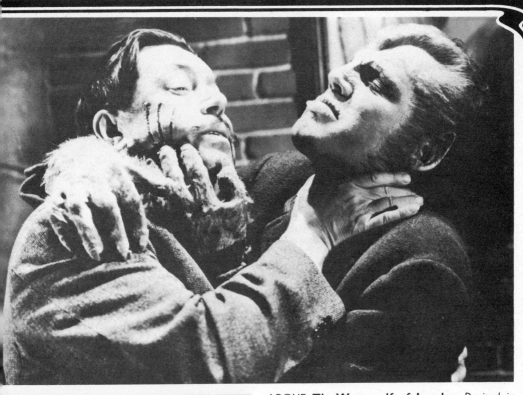

ABOVE **The Werewolf of London** *Devised in 1934 by Universal Studios, where they had a specialist in monstrous make-up called Jack Pierce, this was a disappointingly half-hearted creation. The story derived from a novel by Guy Endore about an unfortunate fellow who developed wolflife characteristics every full moon. The only antidote is a mariphasy flower· which inconveniently blooms only at midnight and only in Tibet. The gentleman on the right, Henry Hull, plays an innocent botanist who, searching for the rare flower, was bitten by the gentleman on the left, Warner Oland, when in his full-fledged werewolf form (rather suggested than shown in the film). Mr Oland has come all the way to London to get the plant back, and why he remains clean-shaven when Mr Hull has turned all hairy is something only the scriptwriters can explain.*

Them! *In the science fiction age of the fifties, monsters had to be caused by man's meddling with things better left alone, e.g. atom bombs. Them ('they'?) in fact were giant ants, bred underground by the effects of atomic radiation, and finally cornered (so they say) in the Los Angeles sewers. Despite the sensational ad, this was a rattling good film, starting with a couple of suspense sequences before the monsters made their appearance, and intelligently scripted throughout. It produced no sequels, but a host of imitations, such as...*

The Black Scorpion, *which used almost the same story but was mainly photographed at night to hide its technical deficiencies. Apart from one rather effective scene in the scorpion's lair, it was flat and unimaginative.*

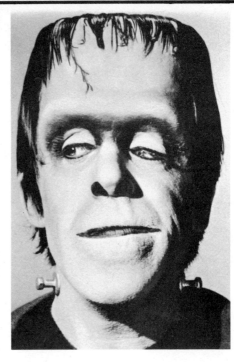

Frankenstein *was not a monster: he was the scientist baron hero of Mary Shelley's book. The thing he created from dead bodies, presumably after the manner of modern heart transplants, was called the Creature in the book, in the 1930 film '??????', and subsequently 'the monster', though most film-goers confused it with its creator and called it Frankenstein. It was the screen's most chilling monster creation, but proved to give the best opportunity for acting, at least in the hands of Boris Karloff, ABOVE LEFT whose eyes admirably reflected hate and suffering. His appearances in the 1931 film are genuinely frightening, instilling a kind of cold hypnotic fear; but by 1935 he has been so humanized (in Bride of Frankenstein) LEFT that after the opening scene he inspires only sympathy, especially when rejected by his specially concocted fiancée. Note that his hair is much greyer now!*

After Karloff retired from the role, the monster was played by Lon Chaney Jnr (Ghost of Franken-stein, 1942), Bela Lugosi (Frankenstein Meets the Wolf Man, 1943) and Glenn Strange (House of Frankenstein, et seq.), but none of them portrayed more than a nasty giant with a funny face. The later Hammer remakes went in solely for charnel-house horror, and in 1965 the monster was played for laughs (by Fred Gwynne) in a TV series called 'The Munsters' ABOVE.

RE-INCARNATED EVIL FROM OUT OF THE MISTS OF PRE-HISTORY

① A NIGHTMARISH AFTERMATH OF A TERROR THAT STALKED ANCIENT GREECE! PERSEUS, TO SAVE HIS MOTHER FROM KING POLYDECTES IS PLEDGED TO BRING HIM THE HIDEOUS SNAKE-WREATHED HEAD OF THE GORGON, MEDUSA, THE SIGHT OF WHICH TURNS MEN TO STONE

ARMED AND INSTRUCTED BY THE GODS, PERSEUS EVENTUALLY DISCOVERS THE GORGON AND HER TWO IMMORTAL SISTERS, MEGAERA & TISIPHONE

② FIXING HIS EYES ON THEIR REFLECTION IN HIS SHIELD, PERSEUS STRIKES OFF MEDUSA'S HEAD WITH A SINGLE BLOW. TAKING THE HEAD IN A MAGIC WALLET, HE MAKES HIS ESCAPE FROM THE TWO REMAINING GORGONS

THE REVENGE OF PERSEUS — TO THE INCREDULOUS TYRANT POLYDECTES AND HIS COMPANIONS, PERSEUS PRESENTS HIS TERRIBLE GIFT... AND THERE THE PETRIFIED FIGURES REMAIN FOR ALL TIME...

...AND OF THE REMAINING GORGONS, NOTHING IS KNOWN UNTIL, CENTURIES LATER, IN THE VILLAGE OF VARNDORF, A SUCCESSION OF MURDERS SHOCKS THE WORLD. ALL THE VICTIMS ARE TURNED TO STONE.!!

① BACKED BY AN AMERICAN SHOWMAN WHO PLANS TO EXHIBIT THE TREASURES OF THE DEAD PHAROAHS IN EUROPE, ARCHAEOLOGISTS OPEN THE TOMB OF THE MURDERED KING RA-ANTEF

② YOU WILL PAY WITH YOUR LIVES

THEY ARE WARNED TH... THIS IS AN ACCURSED ACT BECAUSE...

...THE ANCIENT EGYPTIANS BELIEVED IN THE RESURRECTION OF THE BODY AS MANY PEOPLE STILL DO

④ BUT HOW COULD THE CURSE B... FULFILLED ON THE OTHER SIDE... THE WORLD IN A MODERN CITY THOUSANDS OF YEARS LATER

DON'T MISS TWO OF THE MOST ASTOUNDING VENTURES INTO THE STARKEST UNKNOWN REALMS OF THE SUPERNATUR...

"THE GORGON" and "THE CURSE of the MUMMY'S TOMB" at your local cinema soo...

The Mummy We all know from reading ab... the treasures of Tutankhamun that the Ancie... Egyptians carefully preserved their dead in s... roundings of palatial grandeur. In 1922, a Brit... archaeological expedition uncovered Tutankhamu... tomb, and was subsequently struck with such... series of fatal accidents and illnesses that the... were whispers of an ancient curse. From t... atmosphere derived Hollywood's 1932 mummy fil... about a 3000-year-old gentleman still seeking... reincarnation of his lost love. Karloff played t... role, and did not swathe himself in bandages exce... briefly at the start; for most of the film he j... looked very wrinkled. Oddly enough, the tone of t... film was romantic rather than horrific.

The Gorgon is an unfamiliar monster to most people, so comic strips like the one at the top were devised to give her background when Hammer tried her out in 1964. But her reception was insufficiently encouraging to warrant a sequel, especially as it proved very difficult to keep all those snake heads writhing...

In 1940, and then through the Second World War, Universal spawned a series of increasingly inept second features with first Tom Tyler, then Lon Chaney Jnr, as the avenging mummy, a fearful creature revived on nights of the full moon by a syrup of tanna leaves administered by a faithful priest. Revolting rather than frightening, they were also absurd because the mummy had only one stiff arm with which to strangle his victims, and moved so slowly that even the frailest cripple could have got out of his way had the script not dictated otherwise. In the sixties a British series was made by Hammer: here is Fred Clark gazing at his trophy in Curse of the Mummy's Tomb.

The Golem was the central figure of a story from medieval Jewish mythology, a clay man who would come to life and defend his people when the star of David was placed in a suitable aperture on his chest. The yarn was filmed many times in Europe, best of all in Germany in 1920. The distorted yet recognizably medieval sets were derived from The Cabinet of Dr Caligari and generated not only the middle-European influence in American cinema but the Hollywood horror film cycle which began a decade later. Frankenstein certainly borrowed and adapted from The Golem the scene in which the monster stops in his rampage to make friends with a little girl.

The Invisible Man is only frightening because of camera tricks, when inanimate objects start to move themselves around. The actor was never seen unless swathed in bandages, as Jon Hall is in this scene from The Invisible Man's Revenge (1944) with John Carradine.

The Phantom of the Opera Like King Kong, this Hollywood perennial from a story by Guy Endore is basically a reworking of 'Beauty and the Beast'. A disfigured composer lurks in the sewers below the Paris Opera House, destroying all who get in the way of the innocent young singer who is his protégée. Lon Chaney (senior) got the most out of the role in the splendid 1926 production; the death mask he wore was only surpassed by his real face when in the climactic scene the girl tears off his mask as he sits at the organ.

Dracula is a stately figure based on a mixture of history and mythology stemming from Transylvania, in mist-shrouded central Europe. There was a Count Dracula four hundred years ago, noted for his cruelty; but his name was later tacked on to the local legend of undead people who feast on the blood of the living. Bram Stoker, a Victorian Englishman, worked a splendid Gothic novel out of all this; published in 1897, it has never been out of print. In 1922 came the first film, a pirated German version called Nosferatu, with Max Schreck; eerily photographed, and very effectively close to the book, it added to the legend by having Dracula fade away into nothing when caught out at cockcrow.

Bela Lugosi, ABOVE LEFT appropriately a Hungarian, was Hollywood's first Dracula in 1931 (he had played the role on the stage). He was perfectly splendid but the film was slow and stodgy, having been advertised as 'the strangest love man ever had for woman'. More magical asides were added; the count cast no reflection in mirrors, and when out in search of his nightly prey could change himself into a bat. Lugosi adored the role but played it only twice more; when he died, he asked to be buried in his Dracula cloak.

Other Draculas proliferated. Lon Chaney Jnr BELOW LEFT (Son of Dracula, 1943) called himself Alucard (spell it backward) and could vanish into smoke when cornered. John Carradine (House of Frankenstein, 1944) withered away to a skeleton when exposed to the sun but in House of Dracula reappeared in search of a blood transfusion. Most spectacular disintegration was that of Christopher Lee in the 1958 remake; he turned into ashes, but was later reconstituted by the addition of blood.

Dr Jekyll and Mr Hyde *was created as a long/ short story by Robert Louis Stevenson. Jekyll was a respected doctor experimenting with a drug that would separate the good and evil in man's personality; Hyde was what resulted when Jekyll took the drug himself. Hollywood had to visualize Hyde in a rather corny way, by having poor Jekyll sprout hair and irregular false teeth; but Fredric March in the 1932 version, pictured here FAR RIGHT, won an Academy Award for his performance. Other versions had Hyde handsomer than Jekyll, and in one case Jekyll turned into a beautiful woman! The yarn has been highly popular, attracting such eminent actors as Sheldon Lewis, John Barrymore, Spencer Tracy, Louis Hayward, Boris Karloff, Paul Massie, and Christopher Lee; and in 1953 Hyde was inevitably met by Abbott and Costello RIGHT. We wonder if that really is Boris Karloff under all the make-up?*

The Hunchback of Notre Dame *has one of the most distinguished pedigrees in our gallery, deriving from Victor Hugo's novel* Notre Dame de Paris. *He is no more than physically handicapped, but in medieval days people jeered at the abnormal, so Quasimodo hides in the rafters of the cathedral, where he has grown deaf from his job of bell-ringer. He and his cruel guardian Frollo both covet the gypsy girl Esmeralda, and tragedy results. In 1923 Lon Chaney had a field day in the role; our picture, however, is from the 1939 version with Charles Laughton, who was given such a grotesque make-up that the film's chief publicity gimmick was to hide his face in all the stills. In 1956 the story was refilmed, to little effect, with Anthony Quinn.*

You may have heard the old saying 'the camera cannot lie'. It was never really true of course, even of the still camera, and the movie camera can be made to tell the most incredible stories. Trick films are almost as old as the cinema itself, thanks mainly to a very clever Frenchman named Georges Méliès.

Méliès was a successful stage magician and the director of the Robert Houdin Magic Theatre in Paris, when in 1896 he visited one of the early film shows by the Lumière Brothers. Impressed by what he saw, he decided to include films in his magic programme and soon obtained a movie camera. One day when he was filming some traffic in a Paris street the camera jammed. He managed to free it fairly quickly and carried on filming. A little later, on projecting the film, he was amazed to see a bus instantly and miraculously turn into a hearse. What had happened, of course, was that a bus had been passing at the moment that his camera had jammed. By the time he managed to start filming again the bus had gone and a hearse had taken its place. The result on the screen was that one apparently changed into the other.

Méliès realized that what had happened accidentally could be repeated on purpose and over the next fifteen years he devised most of the camera tricks that are now commonplace, and produced a whole series of brilliantly imaginative and inventive film fantasies that even today are still very entertaining. His films appear even more impressive when you remember that he had none of the sophisticated film-printing techniques which are available to modern filmmakers. Nearly all his tricks (special effects we call them today) had to be achieved by use of the movie camera itself. Such tricks are called 'in camera' effects to distinguish them from those

CAMERA

The father of camera magic Georges Méliès in one of his own films. This is the movies' first example of double exposure being used to allow an actor to appear in two parts in the same scene.

more elaborate effects which are added to a film in the laboratory.

The simplest of the 'in camera' tricks is the one which Méliès first stumbled on accidentally and it can be used to make objects or people appear, disappear or change into something else. Suppose, for instance, that we wish to make a vase of flowers suddenly appear on an empty table. We set the camera up, on a very firm stand or tripod, pointing at an empty table. The table is filmed for a few seconds and the camera stopped. Next, being extra careful not to move the table or the camera we put a vase of flowers on the table and re-start the camera. When the film is projected the audience will not realize that the camera has been stopped and re-started in the middle of the shot, and the vase of flowers will suddenly appear as if by magic. In exactly the same way we can make the flowers vanish or change into a cabbage or whatever we fancy.

like Figure (c), and creates the illusion that the man is walking up a very steep hill. We have to make sure of course that there are no trees or telegraph poles in view as they would appear to lean backwards and thus give the game away.

If you run a movie camera backwards, so that the film travels upwards past the lens, then the film, when it is projected, will show the action in reverse. This is called 'reverse motion' and it is a trick that can be used to produce lots of different effects. At its simplest it can make a ball jump off the floor into someone's hand, or a diver travel backwards out of the water and finish up standing on the diving board. But it can also be used in less obvious ways, so that the audience isn't aware that a camera trick is even taking place. Suppose we want to make a car travel very fast right up to somebody standing or perhaps lying in the road. It is much safer and simpler to start the scene with the car stationary, close up to the person, then have it quickly back away while filming it in reverse motion, with the camera running backwards. Maybe there is a scene in the film in which a knife is thrown, narrowly flashing past the hero's nose and thudding into a door. The dagger is first stuck in the door, a length of black thread is attached to the handle, the actor stands close to it and as soon as the camera starts running, in reverse, the dagger is whipped away.

Films are projected at twenty-four frames or pictures per second, but the camera which takes the film can operate at any speed ranging from four thousand frames per second, in the case of special high speed cameras, right down to one frame per day. Only when the camera speed is the same as the projection speed is movement shown correctly. If we film at four thousand frames per second, one second of real time will take four minutes to project, but at one frame per day a whole year of real time will last only twenty seconds on the screen. These extreme speeds are generally only used for scientific filming, but slow and fast motion filming crops up fairly regularly in lots of films. Half-speed filming at twelve frames per second is often used to speed up car chase sequences, and slow motion speeds of sixty-four pictures per second are sometimes used for sequences in sporting films or to create dreamlike effects.

A slightly more complicated camera trick than those we have mentioned so far is superimposition. This simply means exposing the same piece

MAGIC

Merely tilting a camera can produce a very useful effect. Normally the camera is kept upright, which means that the bottom line of the picture is horizontal, but if the camera is tilted to one side a perfectly flat piece of ground can be made to look like a steep hill. Suppose we set up the camera to photograph a man walking across a flat field. Figure (a) shows what we will see in the camera's viewfinder. If now we tilt the camera over to the right and tell the man to lean forward as he walks, the picture we see in the viewfinder will look like Figure (b). When the film is projected, however, the scene will look

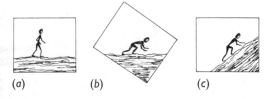

(a)   (b)   (c)

of film twice, which is what happens accidentally in a still camera when you forget to wind on the film and take two separate photographs on the same negative. In films it can be used to make ghosts appear, or to allow an actor to play two parts in the same scene, or merely to put title lettering on top of a scene. To make a ghost appear in a room, first of all the room is filmed with any other actors who may be in the scene; then the film is wound back in the camera, with the lens carefully covered. Next the 'ghost' acts out his part against a black background and is photographed on the same roll of film. When the film is projected the ghost will appear, semi-transparent, in the original room with the other actors who will of course appear quite solid and normal. Superimposing title lettering onto a moving background can be done in exactly the same way. The background is first filmed quite normally. After the film has been wound back in the camera it is then re-exposed on the title, which is printed in white lettering on a matt black card. The final result will show the white letters on top of the moving background scene. Because the letters are white, however, they will appear quite solid and not transparent like the 'ghost' in the previous example. In both cases, the black background used in the second exposure has not registered on the film, so the first

scene photographed is not affected except by the 'ghost' or the white lettering.

The most spectacular 'double exposure' tricks are created by exposing only part of the picture area each time. To do this, various shaped masks are placed in front of the camera lens. Suppose, for instance, that we use a mask to obscure exactly half the lens, and then photograph an actor in a room, making sure that he carefully keeps inside the part of the room seen by the half-covered camera lens. Now we wind back the film, having first made sure that the lens is completely covered up. Now we move the actor to the opposite side of the room and re-

---

Today's great master of screen wizardry is Ray Harryhausen who has been responsible for the special effects in a long line of brilliant fantasy films including Mysterious Island *and* Jason and The Argonauts. *In this scene from his most recent film* The Golden Voyage of Sinbad *a six-armed sword wielding goddess does battle with Sinbad and his crew. In reality the goddess is a small movable model, less than twelve inches tall. It is made to move by a similar technique to that used in cartoon animation. The live actors are filmed separately and the two or sometimes more pieces of film are eventually combined together by a complex printing process called 'travelling matte'.*

In this scene Sinbad encounters another of Ray Harryhausen's fearsome creatures. The models are made of flexible latex rubber which is moulded onto a precision made fully jointed framework or skeleton. This allows the creatures to be moved into any position and then photographed.

position the mask to exactly cover the other half of the lens. We film the actor again and the final result on the film will be to show the one actor apparently playing two parts in the same scene. With careful rehearsal and exact timing he will be able even to carry on a conversation with his other self. Where the two halves of the scene join could cause a vertical line on the picture, so the cameraman usually arranges for this line to coincide with a natural vertical line in the set. This could be the edge of a door frame or the corner of a room.

For simplicity we have described all these tricks as being achieved in the movie camera. In practice, however, in most modern-day film-making, they are more usually done in the film laboratory by means of a very useful piece of equipment called an optical printer. Although precisely made, and therefore very expensive, the optical printer in principle is quite a simple piece of equipment. It consists of a movie camera and a projector pointing towards each other. Both are fastened to a massive base, and the camera is able to slide backwards and forwards, towards or away from the projector, and even sideways. Both camera and projector can be made to run film either forwards or backwards. By using an optical printer many camera tricks can be added to a film after it has been shot. The original film is run through the projector part and is then re-photographed by the camera, at which time any required effects can be added. To superimpose lettering, for example, the background film of a moving scene might be run through the projector and re-photographed by the camera. The film in the camera is wound back and a piece of film containing the white lettering on a black background is now run through the projector and photographed again on the first piece of film. When this film is taken out of the camera and processed, the result will be white lettering printed on top of the moving scene. Film-makers much prefer to use an optical printer to make special effects because it saves a great deal of time during the main shooting in the film studio and gives them much more freedom to decide where and when to include such effects in their films. Today the optical printer is one of the most important tools in the film-maker's kit and it plays some part in virtually every film you see.

Two Fairy Tales and How Hollywood Treated Them

Most new films have a brief period of glory when they are widely publicized, praised or attacked by the critics, and may even cause a few queues. Then they fade from view and often are seen again only when they turn up on television years later. Through the years, however, a comparative handful of films have survived reissue after reissue, delighting new generations and almost attaining the stature of national monuments.

One of these, of course, is *Gone With the Wind*, which you must have heard of even if you haven't seen it. Made in 1939, it has been brought back every four years or so, latterly in wide screen (by cutting the top and bottom off the original image and magnifying it). And another American film made that same year has become even more beloved: *The Wizard of Oz*.

The Wizard of Oz in America is now a television annual. In Britain it is constantly in local cinemas at holiday time, usually on a double bill with *Tom Thumb*. Its simple story is timeless. Dorothy, a little girl who lives in the rather dreary American farming state of Kansas, falls foul of the town's local busybody, Miss Gulch, who wants to have Dorothy's little dog Toto destroyed for barking at her. Discontented already, Dorothy runs away and meets up with a travelling magician, a wise little man who urges her to go back home and face up to things in her own back yard instead of always dreaming of what might lie over the rainbow. Following his advice, she is overtaken by a whirlwind and knocked unconscious. She dreams of being transported to a fairy land of great beauty, where people are extremely kind; but she only wants to get back home. She is told that the only one who can help her is the wonderful wizard of Oz, the Emerald City. Helped and accompanied by a scarecrow, a tin man, and a cowardly lion, she gets there despite the attack of the wicked witch of the west (Miss Gulch). Unfortunately the wizard is a sham, and can offer her no magic, only sound common sense. He offers to take her back home by balloon, but that too fails, and...she wakes up in her own bed vowing never to stray again.

Dorothy, on the yellow brick road to Oz, has befriended a scarecrow, who sings: 'I could while away the hours/Conversin' with the flowers/Consultin' with the rain.../With the thoughts I'd be thinkin'/I could be a second Lincoln/If I only had a brain...' So she takes him with her to ask the all-powerful wizard of Oz for a brain. Then they meet the tin man, who lacks a heart, and joins their quest. The scarecrow is Ray Bolger, the tin man Jack Haley, and the dog is called Toto.

RIGHT *Judy Garland in make-up as Dorothy, the heroine of* The Wizard of Oz. *Does she look twelve years old? She was supposed to be. Actually she turned seventeen during production. In fact, she might have looked younger if her eyebrows had been left more natural, but plucked ones were the fashion in 1939.*

Life is not easy along the yellow brick road, for even the fruit trees turn out to be dangerous agents of the wicked witch of the west, and when Dorothy goes to pick an apple she has to be rescued by her friends.

This cautionary tale full of home truths, an American version of *Alice in Wonderland*, was written by L. Frank Baum and first published in 1902. There had been a silent film version in 1924, and MGM, the biggest and best studio in Hollywood, acquired the rights in the mid-thirties for a remake in colour to fit in with their policy of literary classics (*Treasure Island*, *The Barretts of Wimpole Street*, *The Good Earth*) and commonsensical small-town comedy-dramas such as the successful series with the Hardy family. The most successful child star of the time was Shirley Temple, and of course they wanted her to play Dorothy; but at that time each star was under contract to a studio and Shirley belonged to Twentieth-Century Fox whose boss, Darryl Zanuck, refused to release her. MGM all but abandoned the project, until someone mentioned Judy Garland. Judy was under contract to MGM, so that was all right, but she was going on seventeen: too old, and rather too plump. The rather mad idea was, however, pushed through. They put Judy on a crash diet, dressed her in little girl clothes, and surrounded her with tall actors. In the never-never surroundings of Oz, audiences never thought of her as miscast. Anyway, her voice and personality were just right, and she was helped by a splendid cast of veteran performers, 'old pros' who entered fully into the spirit of the thing.

Looked at critically, *The Wizard of Oz* was

never more than an average production. It has no great style, and the Oz settings seemed a little garish even at the time. But it had an infectious quality that made you like it, helped by a handful of splendid songs: 'If I Only Had a Brain', 'Ding Dong the Witch is Dead', 'Ha Ha Ha, Ho Ho Ho', 'We're Off to See the Wizard'. The most famous song of all nearly got cut before release. Near the beginning of the film Dorothy sings dreamily of her longing for something better and more exciting in life, and

The travellers are joined by a cowardly lion (Bert Lahr, centre), who sings in a suspiciously New Yorkish accent: 'It's sad to be admittin'/I'm as vicious as a kitten/Without the vim and voive.../I could show off my prowess/Be a lion, not a mowess/If I only had the noive.' They all reach the wizard (Frank Morgan) safely, but he turns out to be an imposter who hasn't the magic to help them. Note in this photograph Dorothy's gleaming ruby slippers. They were kept in the studio's prop department for over thirty years, and sold at a 1971 auction for thousands of dollars to a collector for whom the film obviously held many happy memories.

the studio executives decided that the song was too slow and held up the action. Luckily they put it back. It was 'Over the Rainbow', and it became Judy Garland's theme song for the rest of her life.

The film was an instant success. The Second World War was just beginning and this made a fantasy even more acceptable as a contrast to the horrors of real life. 'Over the Rainbow' came to mean the same as 'after the war'. *The Wizard of Oz* was a huge box office success from the word go, which pleased everyone but Darryl Zanuck, who had refused to lend Shirley Temple to star in it. Hearing during pre-production that *Oz* had all the earmarks of a big hit, he determined to outdo it by making his own fairy tale spectacular starring Shirley Temple, then ten years old and the proper age. He hit upon another literary classic, *The Bluebird*, written as a play by a Belgian, Maurice Maeterlinck, in 1915. All he had to do was change the leading character from a boy to a girl, and he was then all set with a property which looked remarkably similar to *Oz*. It was about another discontented little girl, daughter of a poor European woodcutter, who dreamed of finding the bluebird of happiness. A fairy helps her to seek it in the past, in the land of luxury, and in the future, but she finally comes home and finds it in her own back yard, after-wards releasing it so that it can be enjoyed by

Meanwhile Dorothy and her friends have destroyed the wicked witch (Margaret Hamilton) by pouring water over her, and her army of flying monkeys now pays allegiance to Oz.

everyone. On her journey she is helped and accompanied by her treacherous cat and faithful dog, who are changed by the fairy into humans.

Production of *The Bluebird* began, and money was poured into it. Costumes, art work and sets were all of the very best, and it was expected to have all the commercial success of *The Wizard of Oz* plus plenty of prestige as a dignified and effective treatment of a classic. It was given pompous premières, and attempts were made to 'road show' it, that is to show it at separate performances with high prices. Not too un-

expectedly, it flopped. This is a pity, for *The Bluebird* was a film of great quality; but the reasons are not hard to find. It came too soon after *The Wizard of Oz*. The settings were European, not American. It had no songs. Shirley Temple had been a huge box office attraction for five years, and was now on the wane. There were no stars in the supporting cast, and the dialogue was slightly too adult in its implica-tions, even for most adults. Most important, perhaps, the whole production had a slightly 'creepy' feel, rather like those aspects of Grimms' Fairy Tales which are usually glossed over or omitted in children's editions. For instance, when Shirley goes into the past, she starts through the cemetery, and visits her long-dead grandparents, who seem to spend their time sleeping in front of their little rose-covered cottage: they only wake up, they explain, when someone thinks of them. The future is in heaven, where she visits a group of children yet unborn, including one who is to be a great scientist, one who knows he is un-wanted, and another who has been told he will not live long. All through the film there are equally uncomfortable moments: the forest fire sequence is magnificently staged, but one feels it is wrong for the cat, however treacherous, to die in it, especially as Gale Sondergaard has played her with splendid feline majesty.

The Bluebird went the way of all Hollywood's

In gratitude the fake wizard agrees to take Dorothy back home in the air balloon which accidentally brought him over the rainbow years before. There is an accident and it takes off without her, but her adventures have after all been a dream, so all ends happily.

flops: having heralded it with such bravura, Fox now quietly forgot it had ever happened and put it in a vault. It was once reissued in England, around 1949, but has not been seen since. In America when TV came along someone decided it was too long and sliced off the entire introduction sequence, so that the film now begins very abruptly and stupidly with the appearance of the fairy. Even this version, which may be all that remains if the original negative was edited, is not available in Europe, as the literary rights lapsed and are thought by the owners to be not worth renewing.

There we are, then: two fairy tale films made thirty-five years ago. One successful, one not. But success has nothing to do with quality, and one hopes the original negative of *The Bluebird* has been kept in some film archive so that it can be studied in the future, for at its best it was a production of rare craft and delicacy compared with which the jaunty *Wizard of Oz* was a mere comic strip.

ABOVE *Shirley Temple with Johnny Russell in* The Bluebird. *Shirley had the advantage of being just the right age for the role, but the character was rather unsympathetic: Mytyl was selfish and ungrateful.*

BELOW *The children of* The Bluebird *have to find their way to happiness in a most curious way: by visiting the past, through the cemetery. This still gives an idea of the very important part played by lighting to create an effect of spookiness.*

In their travels the children are helped by their faithful dog, turned by the good fairy into a human being. Here is a before and after picture: you must admit there's a resemblance, even though Eddie Collins doesn't seem to think so.

The cat is also transformed into the human shape of Gale Sondergaard; but her advice is not to be trusted, as this still suggests.

Eventually the wanderers arrive in the land of children yet unborn, a pink and blue place in the heavens. But it isn't the home of the bluebird...like Dorothy, they eventually find happiness in their own back yard.

LOOKING INTO THE CRYSTAL BALL

Filmgoing Present and Future

Much of this book has been about the early days of film, or its golden age, which most people agree was the thirties and forties. They were the decades of escapism and optimism, with full cinemas even when half the world was fighting the other, a conflict of right against might. In those dark days people needed the cinema to show them how good life had once been and how some day it might be even better.

That never really happened. Life became more practical and comfortable, but since the Second World War the world has staggered towards problems of increasing gravity and apparent insolubility. At the same time there was a general revolution in living standards amongst what used to be called the working classes. All this has been reflected in cinema films: bitter laughter has had to replace slapstick, family films no longer show typical domestic life, and musicals express an innocence which people feel has no relation to their own personalities.

Concurrently with these world problems, the Hollywood studio system, which had led the way to filmdom's hour of glory, came to an end. The men who had pioneered it retired or died, and their successors were not strong enough, in face of rising costs and the growing difficulty of making films pay in a declining market (young people could now afford a wide range of hobbies instead of automatically crowding to the cinemas), to prevent their power from passing to the actors, who from now on paid the piper and called the tune. Films were set up and made one at a time, a wasteful system compared with the efficiency of the old studios. More and more films were made on real-life locations instead of the studios; again, not always a good idea, as it robbed films of their magic. Nearly everything was shot in colour, of varying quality. New systems like Cinemascope and 3-D were brought in hurriedly in an attempt to halt the decline, but they did so only temporarily and generally caused a setback in film technique.

Added to all these problems came television– the enemy of cinema–which provided pretty good, and increasingly better, entertainment (including those great old movies) for people free of charge in their own homes. And homes had been getting more comfortable. So the only group of people who really wanted to get out at night and go to a movie were the unattached young, the courting couples. To attract them, film-makers tried every kind of sensation, becoming increasingly daring especially towards the end of the sixties. Occasional excellent films have been made to good box office response, but there can never be enough masterpieces or commercial successes (which is seldom the same thing) to keep the industry going as it once was. All over the world cinemas have been greatly reduced in number, and those that remain have often been 'twinned' or 'tripled', forming perhaps three small anonymous cinemas within the shell of the cathedral-like movie palace which once was. In Britain the lowest cost of admission has multiplied about twenty times, from six old pennies to the equivalent of a hundred and twenty (50p), so that for most children a visit to the cinema now has to be restricted to high days and holidays.

For the future, although admissions are still declining, it looks as though the position will stabilize for a few years. After all, a film that 'clicks' can still make a fortune, even though for every one that does about thirty fail miserably; and the day of the blockbuster seems to have passed. (During the sixties many cinemas were re-equipped to take enormously expensive spectacular films shot on wide film, with stereophonic sound, to be shown at advanced prices on a reserved ticket basis. One of them, *Cleopatra*, is said to have cost fifty million dollars. Far too many of them failed even to get their negative costs back.)

It is difficult to feel affection for today's films as one did for their predecessors. Admira-

RIGHT *Epics on the whole continued in the sixties to justify their big budgets, though to secure international appeal some curious decisions were made. In* Khartoum, *for instance, American Charlton Heston played British General Gordon, and British Laurence Olivier, who is thought to lend prestige but not box office appeal to a film, blacked his face to play the Mahdi. The film was a fairly serious and intelligent stab at history, and must have bored some action fans; even so, it invented for dramatic purposes two conversations between the leading characters, who in real life never met.*

LEFT *Epic comedies too were fairly popular. The* Great Race *was a good one, though over-long. It cost millions to make, and was full of slapstick disasters, so one wonders why its advertising is so subdued. Interestingly, it was dedicated to Mr Laurel and Mr Hardy, but few of its routines bore much resemblance to their work. Enjoy it when it turns up on television: such a vast budget is unlikely to be available for any similar project in the seventies.*

RIGHT *Increasingly through the sixties, the name of Alistair Maclean as author came to mean almost as much as James Bond in spelling box-office excitement, and produced good returns for mediocre spy adventures like* Puppet on a Chain *as well as big-scale productions such as* Ice Station Zebra, *which had a highly paid cast battling it out against the unfamiliar backdrop of atomic submarines at the North Pole. The seventies will certainly continue to produce this kind of action fare, but on more careful budgets.*

tion yes–but even looking back at the sixties, many of the most important films seem now to stand in the past like unattractive monuments rather than museum pieces to be revisited with pleasure; they are the productions of aggressive young men asserting themselves rather than the splendidly paradoxical products of an art which was also a craft and an industry. Let us look nevertheless at some well-established types of film and see whether what happened to them in the sixties and early seventies can point the way to their future fate.

Historical and biographical films have become more probing, more subtle and even more cynical than before, from *Lawrence of Arabia* through *Oh What a Lovely War!* to *Young Winston*. Undoubtedly they will go even further in this direction. Science fiction has developed from jolly romps like *The Time Machine* and *First Men in The Moon* to tasteless comic strips like *Barbarella*, clinical suspense thrillers like *The Satan Bug* and *The Andromeda Strain*, sophisticated robot stuff like *Westworld* and the mystic prophecies of *2001: A Space Odyssey*; but the most commercial science fiction idea put on film was *Planet of the Apes*, a basically old-fashioned concept (cf. *Gulliver's Travels*) in which men have become mindless slaves to a race of intelligent monkeys.

The cult of the star seemed to be on the wane, and there is no record of any star even appearing to be responsible for the success of more than two films in a row. On the other hand, loyalty was shown to very old ideas: gangsters were dusted off for fresh use in *Bonnie and Clyde*, *The Godfather* and a hundred imitations; a variety of Shakespeare plays were filmed without much style; dinosaurs and other monster animals were popular in recreations by special effects men like Ray Harryhausen, and the western loped back into popularity via some violent Italian imitations beginning with *A Fistful of Dollars*. The end of the world was contemplated in *Dr Strangelove*, *The Bedford Incident*, *The Day the Fish Came Out* and *The Omega Man*. Horror films got gorier and their twisty plots more repetitive, unleavened by the essential sense of humour. Romances got grottier, especially in the freak *Love Story*, with its tedious foul-mouthed heroine who died

beautifully and painlessly in the best traditions of the thirties. Costume romps with 'X' certificates were given a good send-off by *Tom Jones*, but after poor copies like *Moll Flanders*, *Benjamin* and *Lock Up Your Daughters* the fashion mercifully ceased. We are, however, still suffering from 'problem pictures' in which the main problem is for the audience to ferret out the story, what it means, and whether it has a point: *Blow Up*, *Zabriskie Point*, *The Rain People*, *The Swimmer* and *The Picasso Summer* are examples of this new kind of movie during which the people who pay to be entertained find themselves doing most of the work.

On the whole it was action films which did best, whether the James Bond series which brought a whole new attitude to spies, or solid epics of high adventure such as *Zulu*, *The Professionals*, *Where Eagles Dare* or *The Guns of Navarone*. Audiences have always flocked to cinemas most readily for experiences larger than life, and probably always will.

What of the future? Who knows? Certainly not the film-makers. We write at the end of 1973, a year in which flops and successes have been equally surprising. The box office winners for the year include a couple of sensationally successful hangovers from last year, *Cabaret* and *The Godfather*; three Disney reissue perennials, *Snow White*, *Mary Poppins* and *The Sword in the Stone*; two new action spectaculars, *The Poseidon Adventure* and *The Day of The Jackal*; the latest James Bond; a nostalgic rock musical, *That'll Be the Day*; a TV spin-off, *Love Thy Neighbour*; and examples of fashionable violence in *Last Tango in Paris* and *A Clockwork Orange*. Nothing much there to show the way of things to come, except perhaps that the proportion of successful family films is higher than the proportion actually produced.

Future production plans in Hollywood and London reveal only a state of confusion, a reliance on hit-or-miss decisions. It seems more difficult at this time than at any other in the past twenty years to forecast what kind of films we shall be seeing two or three years ahead. A reaction against violence? A return to cinematic musicals? Eastern westerns? Murder mysteries? Sophisticated comedy? Only time can tell.

Until the sixties the most important ingredient of a film was always the star. Fans had gone dutifully to film after film because Elizabeth Taylor, or Bette Davis, or Clark Gable was billed at the head of the cast. No longer. Nothing, and certainly not a star, can guarantee the success of a picture. Alec Guinness, a world favourite in the fifties, had particularly bad luck in the sixties, when two of his star vehicles foundered in succession without much in the way of a release. This was one of them; but his co-stars will help to make it popular on television.

In the old days, a film which successfully made new departures was always copied shamelessly by other companies, and the imitations would continue to make money for a year or two. In the sixties this could no longer be guaranteed; fans seemed to prefer to pay for continual revivals of the original success than to tolerate pale copies. Moll Flanders, for instance, followed determinedly on the heels of Tom Jones and aped every aspect of it, but died at the box office, whereas Tom Jones continued to be a profitable revival for eight or nine years.

American comedy, on which British cinemas had relied for thirty years, became notably less popular during the sixties, and many of the more sophisticated and better comedies were barely seen at all in the UK after a few days in the West End of London. This may have been because we were breeding our own kind of smart comedy via television, or because television was offering too much American comedy for nothing. A very interesting point in this advertisement is that the two stars could not agree who should take precedence in billing. The final compromise was to have their names cross each other windmill fashion, so that neither can claim to be first.

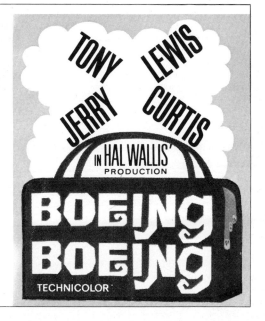

123

Glossary

To explain terms used in this book, some of which may be vague or unfamiliar to you.

ABSTRACT FILM One in which the pictures do not represent familiar scenes but fall into visually interesting or significant patterns, e.g. *Yellow Submarine*, parts of *Fantasia*.

ACADEMY AWARDS Prizes given annually since 1927 by the Hollywood Academy of Motion Picture Arts and Sciences, whose members vote for the 'best of the year' within various categories. The award takes the form of a statuette known, for a reason which remains mysterious, as Oscar. In Britain, the Society of Film and Television Arts makes similar awards, but they do not have the same news value.

ACTION STILL A photograph of a scene as it actually appears in the film, rather than one posed after filming. Hundreds of 'stills', for publicity purposes, are made of each film.

ANAMORPHIC LENS One which compresses a wide range of action into normal 35-mm film; a complementary lens in the projector can then expand it to fill a wide CinemaScope or Panavision screen.

ANIMATION The filming of static drawings, puppets or other objects in sequence so as to give an illusion of movement. Sometimes called STOP FRAME ANIMATION because only one frame of film is exposed at a time, the objects then being slightly rearranged before the next shot.

ARC A high-powered lamp used in projectors and studio lighting, its illumination consisting of an electrical discharge between two carbon rods.

ASPECT RATIO The shape of the screen as you look at it, expressed in its relative breadth and height. For instance, 4:3 would be the aspect ratio of a screen four feet wide and three feet high, also of a screen forty feet wide and thirty feet high. 4:3 was in fact the standard ratio until 1952, when 'wide' screens were produced by cutting off the top and bottom of the image to produce a ratio of about 5:3. CinemaScope and other anamorphic (qv) processes are projected at about 7:3. The TV screen is fixed at the old ratio of 4:3, so that all wide screen films lose something when played on it.

BACKLOT The garden area of a film studio, in which houses, railway stations, city streets, etc, are often built amid natural surroundings.

BACK PROJECTION A method of producing location sequences in the studio by placing actors before a translucent screen onto which a previously filmed scenic background is projected.

BALLYHOO An expressive word denoting the kind of wild publicity which has little to do with the merits, or indeed the contents, of the film in question.

BILLING The credits of a film as presented to the public; a producer concerned about his billing fears that the combination of stars, title, etc is less attractive than it might be.

BIOPIC A contraction for biographical picture.

BLOOP To cover a join in the sound track, usually with thick 'blooping ink'.

BLOW UP To magnify an image, either a photograph for background purposes, or a piece of film from, say, 16-mm to 35-mm.

BOOM A 'long arm' extending above the camera unit and carrying a microphone which can be balanced over the actors so that sound is picked up even in a semi-distant shot. A 'camera boom' is a high moveable platform strong enough to carry the entire camera unit.

CINEMASCOPE A wide screen process using an anamorphic lens (qv).

CLAPPERBOARD A hinged board recording the details of each shot. As the director calls 'action', the two halves of the board are clapped together, forming an easily recognizable bang on the sound track to be married up with the start of picture action.

CO-FEATURE A film designed, or fated, to be shown in cinemas as half a bill, and therefore deserving only half the takings. Normally three-quarters or more will go to the main feature, and almost nothing to the support.

CONTINUITY The development of cinematic narrative from the beginning to the end of a film. If continuity is good, the audience will be carried smoothly from one scene to another without realizing the efficiency of the technique.

CREDITS Titles at beginning or end of film (or often these days five minutes after the beginning) listing the creative talents involved.

CUT Noun: an abrupt transition from one scene to another, the first being instantaneously replaced by the second. Verb: to edit a film, or (during production) to stop the cameras turning on a scene.

CUTTING COPY The first print assembled from the 'rushes', sometimes known as a rough cut. When it is considered satisfactory, the negative will be cut to match it, and release prints made.

DEEP FOCUS A kind of cinematography which keeps both foreground and background objects in constant focus. Its effect is generally melodramatic, as in *Citizen Kane*.

DIRECTOR The executive responsible primarily for telling the actors and cameraman what to do in a scene, but also, usually, for the whole creative 'feel' of a picture.

DISSOLVE A change of scene accompanied by gradually exposing a second image while fading the first away.

DISTRIBUTOR A company which, for a percentage of the 'take', sells completed films to cinemas.

DOLLY A trolley, sometimes mounted on rails, on which a camera unit can move in any required direction.

DOUBLE-HEADED PRINT One on which sound and picture are recorded on separate pieces of film, usually at cutting copy stage before OK is received to make combined negative.

DUBBING A word with several shades of meaning, all involving adding sound to picture. Sometimes effects, music and dialogue are added to picture already shot; sometimes a star's poor singing voice is re-recorded with a professional singer to whose voice the star mouths; sometimes the original language is replaced by a translation and entirely different voices.

DUPE NEGATIVE One made from the original (via a fine grain print) to protect it from wear.

EDITOR Technician who assembles final print of film from various tracks and scenes available; except in routine pictures, he works closely to the director's instructions.

ESTABLISHING SHOT Opening shot of sequence, showing location of action.

EXPRESSIONISM The fullest utilization of cinematic resources to give a dramatic, larger-than-life effect, as in *Citizen Kane* and *The Third Man*.

EXTRA A crowd player who has no lines to speak.

FADE IN Gradual emergence of a scene from blackness to full definition; opposite of FADE OUT.

FEATURE FILM Normally accepted to mean a fictional entertainment of more than 3000 feet (34 minutes). Anything less is technically a short. NB. In journalism and television a 'feature' usually means a *non*-fiction article or documentary.

FINE GRAIN PRINT One of high quality stock, used for the making of dupe negatives.

FLASHBACK A break in chronological narrative during which we are shown past events having a bearing on the present situation. *Citizen Kane* consists almost entirely of flashbacks.

FOOTAGE The length of a film expressed in feet.

FRAME A single picture on a strip of film. At normal projection speed, 24 frames are shown each second.

GLASS SHOT A trick shot, usually scenic, in which a feature which does not exist (e.g. a medieval castle required on a hillside actually bare) is painted on a glass slide fixed in front of the lens.

GRIP The technician who builds or arranges the film set. The foreman is usually credited as KEY GRIP.

HARD TICKET A reserved seat.

IMPRESSIONISM Building up a sequence from short disconnected shots, in order to make a point or create an effect (e.g. a dream sequence).

INSERT SHOT One cut into a dramatic scene in order to give the audience a closer look at the subject of attention (e.g. a newspaper headline).

IRIS An adjustable diaphragm on the camera which opens or closes from black like an expanding or contracting circle, giving a similar effect on the screen.

LEADER Length of blank film joined to the beginning of a reel for lacing through the projector. 'Academy' leaders are always placed next to the opening shot: they give a numbered countdown to the start of action.

LIBRARY SHOT One hired to save the expense of shooting it; e.g. plane taking off, train in motion, historical event.

LONG SHOT One taken from a distance, usually to establish a scene or situation but sometimes for dramatic effect.

MASK A technical device for blacking out part of the image, usually to concentrate the attention on what remains. MASKING is the black fabric which surrounds a cinema screen, usually adjustable to encompass the variety of aspect ratios.

MATT A technique, more sophisticated than back projection, for blending actors in the studio with location or trick scenes. The actor is photographed against a non-reflective background (e.g. black velvet) and a negative of this image is combined with one of the desired background. Thus men can move among monsters, and ghosts can slowly disappear. (Also spelt MATTE.)

NEW WAVE A rather meaningless description applied by themselves to a group of exploring French directors in the 1950s: Truffaut, Chabrol, Godard, etc.

NICKELODEON A humorous term applied to early American cinemas when they had become slightly grander than the converted shops in use at the turn of the century.

OPTICALS A general term including all the visual tricks which involve laboratory work: wipes, dissolves, matts, etc.

PAN A shot in which the camera moves or rotates horizontally, e.g. from side to side of a room. A ZIP PAN speeds up the movement into a blur.

POST-SYNCHRONIZATION Adding sound to visuals already shot. Speech can seldom be satisfactorily recorded at the time of shooting because of extraneous noise and special requirements of volume, pitch, etc.

PRODUCER The man in control of the budget and all personnel, including the director; often also the man with the vision of what the completed film should be.

REEL A loose term generally taken to mean one thousand feet of film, which in 35-mm would run just over ten minutes; but these days projectors take up to 5,000 feet.

ROUGH CUT See CUTTING COPY.

RUNNING SPEED In silent days, when projectors had variable speeds, films were designed to run at 16–20 frames per second. The requirements of sound produced new projectors using a standard speed of 24 frames per second. (Television runs at 25 frames per second.) No sound projector can operate at the silent speeds, which is why silent films look jerky when you see them.

SCORE The music composed for a film.

SOFT FOCUS A diffused effect much favoured by ageing film stars: it makes them look glamorous while erasing the ravages of time.

STAR An actor billed above the title, or whose presence is thought likely to draw patrons.

STOCK SHOT See library shot.

SYNCHRONIZATION Marriage of voices to lip movements.

TAKE A single recording of a scene during the making of a film. Sometimes up to fifty takes are necessary to get the desired effect.

TEASER Originally a piece of publicity whipping up interest for a film without actually saying what it is. More recently applied to the piece of action which precedes credit titles.

TELEPHOTO LENS One which brings far-off objects apparently very close, but has the disadvantage of flattening and distorting perspective.

3-D In the thirties and fifties several films were made using the principle of showing two separate images of the same scene, corresponding to the differing angles of our two eyes; when viewed through special glasses which allowed each eye to see only one image, the illusion of normal depth was given, so that objects could approach very convincingly towards one from the screen. The normal film does not give this effect because it is shot through one camera 'eye'. 3-D films did not last because the machinery was subject to breakdown and the glasses were tiresome.

TRACKING SHOT One in which the camera follows the object of interest.

VISTAVISION A method of producing high definition on the bigger screens of the fifties, by using extra wide stock and reducing it to 35-mm during printing.

WIDE SCREEN See ASPECT RATIO.

WIPE An optical device used for quick changes of scene. A line appears at one corner or edge and 'wipes' across, bringing the new picture with it; or more complex patterns such as expanding stars can be devised.

ZIP PAN See PAN.

ZOOM LENS One of variable length, normally used for swiftly magnifying a distant object (so that one apparently zooms toward it) or moving rapidly away from a close one.

ENDPAPER

A happy scene which is also sad. It was taken in 1944, when Metro-Goldwyn-Mayer had been a successful film company for twenty years and were at the height of their success. Little Margaret O'Brien was chosen to cut the cake not only because she was a popular star of the time but also because she symbolized the youth and vigour of the company. Now, alas, she is all but forgotten, and seldom acts, while MGM, after years of indecision, has virtually bowed out of the business and has invested its assets in a Las Vegas complex named after one of its most famous films, Grand Hotel.